A Time to Die

by

WILLIAM PURCELL

Canon Emeritus of Worcester

MOWBRAYS
LONDON & OXFORD

© William Purcell

ISBN 0 264 66320 9

First published in 1978 by
A.R. Mowbray & Co Ltd
Saint Thomas House Becket Street
Oxford OX1 1SJ

Printed in Great Britain by
Fletcher & Son Ltd, Norwich

IN MEMORIAM
WILLIAM BARCLAY

A great teacher to whom I have owed much over the years.

Death is a mystery very full of awe, and yet very full of blessedness. We shall soon know it better; but meanwhile let us gaze calmly upon it; for assuredly the more we do so, the less of awe and the more of blessedness we shall see in it.

BISHOP WALSHAM HOW

Jesus's resurrection is the ground of hope in the resurrection of all who believe in him. Since he is risen, they too will rise.

HANS KUNG: *On Being a Christian*

CONTENTS

PROLOGUE

'It's been such a shock'. The speaker was a woman who had recently lost her husband. He had retired. They had made many plans for what they would do together. And then he had died. Suddenly, there seemed nothing left, because this was the one thing they had not planned for. So it was, for her, as if something absolutely extraordinary had taken place: unexpected, baffling, overwhelming. And yet, as an intelligent woman, she must have known that death was far from being an unusual event. But her shock was utterly genuine, and made it all the more difficult for her to face up to the situation.

This is happening to somebody every day. They are being ambushed by death. It springs out upon the little caravan of their affairs peacefully moving along life's road, with shattering effect all the greater because they are unprepared. Death and bereavement surprise in proportion as they have not been thought about. They shock in proportion as they are un-expected. And they desolate because they present a situation in which, short of self deception, there seems to be no hope except that offered by the slow anaesthesia of time, dulling by degrees the sharpness of grief.

But such a bleak situation need not arise: certainly need not be accepted. Sorrow there will always be, and naturally so. But hopelessness vanishes where there is brought to bear upon it, like sunshine upon darkness, the christian hope of the life of the world to come. How profoundly significant it is that the first of the resurrection appearances of Jesus in St John's Gospel took place 'while it was still dark'! There is Mary of Magdala looking for the tomb in that strange hour when the birds are just stirring and the outline of things is still dim. She finds the tomb with the stone moved away from the entrance. She runs to Simon Peter and 'the other disciple whom Jesus loved' and they discover the tomb empty. Then she is left alone until, the light growing stronger, she discovers Jesus himself in the garden, and he greets her by her name. As the Te Deum says: 'When thou hadst overcome the sharpness of death thou didst open the kingdom of heaven to all believers'. So it can be with all who have 'joy and peace in believing'.

But not all, or even a majority nowadays, perhaps not more than a minority of those whom death overtakes, have anything like this assurance. There are many Christians themselves who, according to frequent opinion polls on this subject seem either tentative or doubtful concerning this christian hope. Thus Malcolm Muggeridge in a feature on 'Death

6

Wishes' in a Sunday paper: 'One just has to suspend judgement. It is part of a larger explanation and it is impossible to know what that is. We must take it on trust. I believe in life after death and I believe that the relationships we have here on earth will be involved'.

But the Scriptures are more explicit than that, as we shall see. The christian hope is that death is not so much an end as a beginning, passing on to a further stage of experience: in other words, to 'the life of the word to come'. It should never be forgotten, however, that this is hope, not knowledge: an act of faith, not the bland acceptance of a certainty. As an act of faith, it is all the more challenging. But the faith is very strongly supported by the testimony of the Scriptures and experience.

There are, now as ever, two major reasons why Christians need to be clear as to what their faith has to say about death, in all its aspects. The first is that they may be able to have a message for those whom death and bereavement have touched. The second is that they may be able themselves to look death in the eye, knowing that he will come for them, as for others, in due time. 'Neither the sun nor death can be looked at with a steady eye', said Le Rochefoucauld. As regards the second, that is not necessarily true. It depends on who is looking. The man of faith can certainly look death in the eye. When his captors came to take to execution that great Christian and patriot, Dietrich Bonhoeffer, in the spring of 1945, he said, in a message to his English friend Bishop Bell: 'for me this is the end; but also the beginning'. And daily, in far less dramatic circumstances, there are many ordinary Christians who, because of their faith, are able to face up with quiet courage to their earthly end.

So to be able to have something of this assurance in one's self, and above all, to be able to communicate something of it to those in need at the time of their need, is a very great thing. Rarely has it been more needed than now, when an increasingly secular world finds itself particularly vulnerable at this point. Sophistication stops short, and becomes a child again, at this frontier. One of the most treasured memories of the writer of these words is that of having had the privilege of being, at his final moments, with a man who in his day had been a distinguished physician. As he was dying he whispered: 'I want to hear what you have to say'. He listened with profound attention to a reading of John 14: 'Set your troubled hearts at rest. Trust in God always; trust also in me. There are many dwelling places in my Father's house . . .', joined in the Lord's Prayer, and then, during a brief commendatory prayer, quietly died. So came to his end, in dignity and in peace, a man who in his time had stood by many beds but who eventually, as is the inevitable lot of human kind, high or low, had been brought to his own, at the last.

Death certainly deserves more than the furtive cover-up treatment it receives in the current world.

This is all the more odd since, in most other personal matters, sex, birth and the like, this must be one of the more outspoken ages that ever was. It has long been taken for granted that in these areas of experience frankness is good and concealment either unnecessary or bad. Birth itself, as a process, is on exhibition, thanks to television. But in the matter of death people still tend either to close up like clams, or pretend it isn't there. One consequence is that many are still, as regards emotional adjustment to this basic factor in human life, quite unprepared for its impact.

Some of the reasons are obvious enough. Most of us live in towns, no longer in contact with the ancient cycle of birth and death, natural as the seasons. So death is concealed and, where there is no sense of community, as in a great city, often lonely. And the fact that, taking place in hospital, it is usually a smoothly processed affair, means that the concealment which goes with it reinforces the conspiracy of silence. An extreme example of this came in a television documentary which showed the special trolley, disguised as an ordinary piece of ward equipment, for the surreptitious removal of a body in such a manner that other patients would not be disturbed. Poor death, to have declined so far in social acceptability!

But there is a more serious aspect to the matter. It is the weakness of the christian voice in this area. The progressive erosion of old hopes and beliefs never

9

matters more than when it emerges as a factor in modern death. Even when some honest piece of investigative journalism, such as that programme which exhibited the camouflaged trolley, seeks to present some of the facts, the christian message is too rarely heard with power. This was not always so. 'O death where is your victory?' asks Paul: 'O death, where is your sting?'. And he adds; 'God be praised, he gives us the victory through our Lord Jesus Christ'. (1Corinthians 15:55:57).

That is the heart of the matter; that ringing confidence. It can be heard in christian voices all down the ages, from all sorts and conditions of people. There is the stunning passage in *Pilgrim's Progress* where Bunyan, having described Christian's entry into the waters of death, a river which he must cross, and alone, before reaching the splendours beyond, says 'so he passed over, and all the trumpets sounded for him on the other side'. Much less well known is a conversation which Archbishop William Temple had with the atheist philosopher Bertrand Russell. They had been talking of the hope of the life to come. Russell naturally denied the validity of any such notion. Temple, a philosopher of equal standing himself, replied: 'There is nothing in the world of which I feel so certain. I have no idea what it would be like, and I am glad I have not, as I am sure that it would be wrong. I do not want it for myself as mere continuance; but I want it for my understanding of life . . . "God is Love" appears to me nonsense in view of the world he has made, if there is no other.'

So, there are these two reasons why the Christian needs to be clear as to the message of his faith about death: to be able to help others in their time of need, and to strengthen himself all the days of his life until 'the shadows lengthen and the evening comes, and the busy world is hushed, the fever of life is over, and our work is done'.

But there is more involved in this, and far sharper challenges presented than that of being only a transmitter of the christian hope, valuable as that is. 'Death has two faces', says Axel Munthe, in *The Story of San Michel* 'and one of them is terrible'. He was speaking, as a doctor, to a mother who wished to keep by her the body of a child who looked so peaceful in his last sleep. The grim note is salutary. Death means decay of this mortal body. Death is no passing pang to be soothed by anodynes. Death is frequently tragic and appealing, as when a car kills a child, or when a husband or wife is struck down by a mortal illness or lost by apparently pointless misadventure. Everybody can produce easily enough their own stories of tragedies. The people of Middle Ages, who lived surrounded by mortality in their crude and cruel world of plague and violence, had a profound respect for death as a formidable adversary. Indeed, for St Paul, death is still the last enemy, and he is still the last enemy now. Albrecht Durer, the fifteenth century German artist expressed the feeling unforgettably in a drawing of two lovers hand in hand in a garden, unseeing of the horrific figure peering out at them from behind a nearby tree — Death, already claiming them for his own. But nothing which the Middle Ages could depict in this line exceeds the starkness of many happenings in our own world. They had their plagues. We have our cancers. And what should be, what could be, the christian message, to the parents of a son written off in a motorway fog pile-up?

That is not a rhetorical question. There is a message to be given, and a high and hopeful one. What needs to be understood is that it is constantly under test, and has often to survive in highly hostile environments, as when people are embittered by grief, and the old, old but ever new questions come tumbling out; 'Why did God allow this to happen?', 'What is the reason for it?', 'Shall we meet again?'. And also there is the ever recurring query; 'What shall I do?'.

Now that is a good question. It opens up a whole new area of christian helpfulness over and beyond, but certainly not above, the offering of faith-based hope and comfort. Death after all, is a total experience, having many facets. There is, to start with, dying; the necessary preliminary, yet an experience in itself. What is dying, how does it seem from the viewpoint of the person concerned, as well as from that of the onlooker? Medicine, history and experience have a lot to tell us here. How are we, the living, to offer companship and support to those approaching that exit through which we ourselves must pass, sometime, some day?

Valuable indeed is then the Christian who, from the standpoint of his faith and out of knowledge gained by previous thought upon the matter, can offer a very present help in trouble. It is wise to think of death, as the natural course of events, beforehand, not only that we may help others; but that we may be able ourselves to adjust to it. As John Donne wrote:

Since I am coming to that holy room,
Where, with the choir of saints for evermore,
I shall be made thy music. As I come,
I tune the instrument here at the door,
And what I must do then, think here before.

There is another side, also, to that cry of the bereaved: 'What shall I do?'. The fact is that, following a death there are, quite simply, many things to be done; practical things, such as contacting an undertaker, arranging the funeral, sorting out legal affairs, planning the necessary re-adjustment to life which must ensue. What is more, the greater the extent to which the bereaved are involved in these nuts and bolts of the situation, the better for them, and for all concerned. The modern habit of placing the bereaved in a ghetto, while various hired specialists arrange everything, is bad practice psychologically and spiritually. People need to be involved in the whole of death, not a few selected parts of it such as the signing of some forms and attendance at a pre-arranged, pre-packaged and often unintelligible funeral service.

Christians follow a Saviour who was made man; who lived as one, and died as one. The earthy consequences of this earthly life are therefore very much his concern, and no friend of his should be hesitant in being involved in them, and in his name. There have been many books about life after death. There have been few which combine with this a concern for the practical aspects of the death which must precede the hope of that new life. The whole experience, as a consequence, gets shorn off at the roots, and the christian hope given the isolated and ephemeral existence of a cut flower.

This need not be so. Death needs looking at steadily and whole. It is a deeply rewarding exercise, and a godly one. The greatest of the rewards is that it helps us to go with confidence into the quite unnecessarily darkened room in which death and its attendant phenomena, like props for an occasionally performed mystery plan, are usually stored. The need is to switch on the light. Then everything looks different: real, honest, interesting; instead of false, evasive and 'untrue. So to do that is the main purpose of this book: to turn on the light.

But before that it is necessary to turn on the power. And to do that it is needful to go to the source of supply, which is the christian hope of the life of the world to come.

THE CHRISTIAN HOPE

Now faith is the assurance of things hoped for, the conviction of things not seen.

Hebrews 11:1

The Love of God

We begin with a collection of family photographs, of the sort which anyone has. There they are, reaching from today, to yesterday, to the day before yesterday. Here are the children. And here are some of us as children ourselves, and then again as young people, and then again, maybe, newly marrieds. Wedding pictures offer a good subject for meditation upon the passage of time and the mystery of human life.

Observe the parents of the bride and groom on that cheerful day; the older generation, already showing signs of their years. If we, who are now looking at these pictures, are ourselves getting on, then that older generation will as like as not have vanished already from the scene. We can still in memory faintly hear their voices, and in the mind's eye hold blurring glimpses of their faces. But that is all. The rest is silence. Whatever age we are when we look at the past we shall soon be a part of it ourselves, just as they are. The great question is; where have they gone, and where shall we ourselves go?

We are able to ask that question because, of all

living creatures, we are alone in possessing foreknow-ledge of our deaths. That is why men have been asking questions about it since the dawn of time. 'Lord, let me know my end,' says the writer of Psalm 39, 'And what is the measure of my days; let me know how fleeting my life is!' And the sombre certainty of mortality is echoed in Ecclesiastes: 'For everything there is a season, and a time for every matter under Heaven: a time to be born, a time to die . . .' (Ecclesiastes 3:1.)

The mystery of it all expands the more it is thought about, and the further we look into the past. Take, for instance, some of those strictly posed studio portraits of the early days of photography, much older than those colour prints we were thinking of a moment ago. What on earth has happened to the people in them all? The one thing which can be said with absolute certainty is that they have gone. And so it was with the generations before them, and then before them, and so on, and so on, into 'the dark backward and abysm of time'. This is the great mystery of human mortality, and this is what the christian hope is about.

What men and women have always wanted to know about the dead - and about themselves when they join them - is whether they are utterly obliter-ated when their physical bodies are worn out or destroyed by sickness or accident, or whether they have some continuing existence. For the Christian, the hope of that is based upon Jesus, the conqueror of death and opener of the way to eternal life and hereafter for his followers.

Man had always, from his earliest beginnings, resisted the idea of total obliteration. That can, of course, always be called wish fulfilment. Few of us find it easy to accept the idea of what, for instance, a recent agnostic writer, Raymond Fletcher M.P. in a letter to the Times described, talking of death, as 'a change of bio-chemical condition to be seen through with as little fuss as possible', and beyond it nothing. No human society has ever yet universally held such a view. On the contrary, human societies from the primitive to the highly complex have held the belief that those who die travel elsewhere, to 'that bourne from which no traveller returns'.

From this came the primitive practices of providing the dead with food for their journey into the unknown, to which the objects - utensils, cooking vessels and the like - found in ancient burial mounds still bear witness. Nor does this kind of belief belong only to the past. Some people, it is true, will in theory subscribe to the view that death is indeed just 'a change in bio-chemical condition' leading to nothing. But it is surprising how many, when faced with the event, will speak and act as they it were more, and that those whom they have loved have a continuing reality.

Yet this feeling, stubbornly held in so many different forms through so many ages, could be called little more than a gut reaction against the intolerable idea that death closes all accounts for ever. Such a concept carries with it also an acceptance of the bleak conclusion that nothing in this world has an extension beyond this life. This means that whatever we have been, or have suffered, or have striven after, or have sacrificed for, is all equally meaningless, thus making of life 'a tale told by an idiot, full of sound and fury, signifying nothing'. Some have found it possible to face the prospect calmly. Many other people have not thought about it at all, and prefer not to. But to many others, in all ages, it just has not made sense. Nor has it to some of the world's greatest minds. When Socrates had been condemned to death he said to his friends, as he left the court: 'Now it is time we were going: I to die and you to live: but which of us has the happier prospect is unknown to anyone but God'.

And so we come to the name at the heart and centre of all our hopes — God. It is in Him and with Him that all our thoughts and hopes about death and the beyond must begin. The answer to why it has never seemed to make sense that death is the end of all things is that such a notion seems widely at variance with the very idea of a loving God who, having willed the lives of men and women in his world, should, age after age, allow them to come to nothing. William Barclay, that great teacher who has himself passed on since this book was begun, put it like this in his autobiography, *Testament of Faith:* 'I think that the best proof that God cares is the existence of the world. I think that we could argue that for the God revealed to men by Jesus Christ the act of creation was a necessity of his being. If God is love, then God must have someone to love. Love cannot exist by itself; and it must go out to someone. Therefore in order to complete himself God had to create a world which he could love and which would love him . God took the risk which love always takes, the risk of rejection. If God had only power, light, knowledge there would have been no world, because there would have been no necessity for a world; it is because God is love that God is also creator.'

The truth that God is a loving God is one which has been discovered over the centuries. It took a long time to evolve. There was a time, as the Old Testament makes clear, when those who worshipped God also feared him. 'We shall surely die, for we have seen God'. (Judges 13:22). What a world of difference between this primitive idea of God, and the beautiful picture, written centuries later, of the God who, in Eden, 'walked in the garden in the cool of the day' and called on Adam by his name. It is the same God who called Abraham to be his friend and confidant; 'Shall I hide from Abraham that thing which I do?' (Genesis 18:17). Moses, again, is one to whom God speaks as a friend (Exodus 33:11). At the same time he is, this same God, great and mighty, proclaiming himself 'merciful and gracious, long suffering, and abundant in goodness and truth'. (Exodus 34:6). Again, this is the same God who is revealed in the Prophets as one who loves righteousness, justice, mercy and forgiveness - all the highest moral qualities - and ordinary men and women too. So the discovery that God is love was not made easily or quickly; but out of a long process or development and revelation. It is a very marvellous thing, of huge significance for all of us personally. God is, and he loves us. And because he loves us, he will not ever want to throw us away. William Temple once said 'The hope of immortality is strictly dependant on faith in God. If God is love immortality follows as a consequence. He made me, he will not let me perish, so long as there is anything in me that he can love'.

But we have to be able to feel this truth of the loving nature of God; it is not enough only to know it. We have to be able to feel that God is truly with us, and knows about us, as we go through our little lives. Unless we can pray, then God seems too far away for human comfort. Studdert-Kennedy expressed this with the poet's tongue when he wrote:

Thou who dost dwell in depths of timeless being,
Watching the years as moments passing by,
Seeing the things that lie beyond our seeing,
Constant, unchanged, as aeons dawn and die;
Thou who canst count the stars upon their courses,
Holding them all in the hollow of thy hand,
Lord of the world with its myriad of forces
Seeing the hills as single grains of sand . . .
Dost thou not see the helpless sparrows falling?
Canst thou not see the tears that women weep?

Canst thou not hear thy little children calling?
Dost thou not watch above them as they sleep?
Then, oh my God, thou art too great to love me,
Since thou dost reign beyond the reach of tears,
Calm and serene as the cruel stars above me,
High and remote from human hopes and fears.

What he is saying is this: how can so distant a God, creator of all that is, even though his nature were loving, be personally concerned with our little lives and what becomes of them? What we need is a more closely focussed hope that death is not the end. We need a hope grounded in a person who lived our human life, in this perishable body, as we do, and whose words and witness are on record, and are a living experience for many, still. We have that hope. We can find such a person in Jesus Christ. We can find, too, that not only what he did and said, but also what happened to him, are of vital importance. That is why Studdert Kennedy ended his poem:

Only in him can I find a home to hide me,
Who on the cross was slain to rise again;
Only with him, my comrade God, beside me,
Can I go forth to war with sin and pain.

The Message of The New Testament

How did Jesus himself think of God? Those who find a difficulty of squaring the idea of a God who

21

can be at one and the same time fashioner of everything from the stars to the atom, with one who also cares about us, the answer is comforting. Jesus thought of God as a father. He called him 'Abba, Father', and it is to him that he cries out in the Garden of Gethsemene before his death. (Mark 14:36). There is a passage in Paul's letter to the Christians in Galatia which brings this out. 'To prove that you are sons God has sent into our hearts the spirit of his son, crying "Abba!, Father!" '.

William Neil has an apt note on this in his commentary on Galatians: 'We are not now dealing with the unpredictable effects of the stars on our destinies, or with a remote and forbidding lawgiver with inexorable demands, but with one who is still author and creator of all that is, but whom we can ever call our dear father. The word Abba brings us very close to Jesus. It is the Aramaic word for father which he used in his own prayers. It is what a Jewish boy would have affectionately called his own father. Jesus has taught us, in stories like the Prodigal Son, to think of God in just this way'.

Jesus never questioned the reality of the life of the world to come. He never argued for its existence. He accepted it as a fact. More importantly, Jesus comes through the Gospels as one who, in a strange way, was himself life. As he is depicted in St John he is from the beginning of things: 'All that came to be was alive with his life, and that life was the light of men. The light shines on in the dark, and the darkness

22

has never quenched it'. (John 1:4). He is the master of all life and gives it in abundance. 'I have come that men may have life, and may have it in all its fulness'. (John 10:10). 'I am the way; I am the truth and I am life' he says in answer to a troubled question of his disciple, Thomas. He says of himself, too, 'I am the resurrection, and I am life. If a man has faith in me, even though he die, he shall come to life; and no one who is alive and has faith shall ever die'. (John 14:25).

These are loaded and mysterious words. They are loaded with many layers of meaning, and they are mysterious because no one has ever understood them fully or, maybe, could hope to in this life. What matters is the continuous thread running through them indicative of the fact that Jesus has something tremendous and momentous to say about life in its relation to death. The main burden of the message is that he, who is life, offers those who choose to follow him a share in this destiny, and with others, the promise of his companionship. John's Gospel uses many metaphors to express this message. 'I am the light of the world. No follower of mine shall wander in the dark'. (John 8:12). He tells the Samaritan woman drawing water at the well that he, to those who will drink of the water which he has to give will be 'an inner spring welling up for eternal life'. (John 4:14). He is the bread of life: He gives the power to live by him as he lives by the Father (John 6.27-58). Whoever lives and believes in him shall not die. (John 11.25).

The message is to those who believe in Jesus, who accept him as Lord, and who choose to try, as best they may to follow him. What Jesus asks of them, when he thus calls them to follow him wherever the way may lead, even through suffering and death, he himself does first. Freely, and because of love for the Father and for his own followers, he gives his life as the good sheperd lays down his life for the sheep (John 10.11). But he thus gives his life in order to take it up again (John 10.17). Afterwards he becomes 'A life giving spirit' (1 Cor 15.45), as Paul says capable of bestowing the gift of life on all who believe in him.

But what kind of life are we talking about? What we are not talking about is any idea of universal immortality. When death moves people to hope about a continuation of the life of someone they have loved, stirring the expectation of meeting them again, it is natural enough to think in this way. But this is not the christian hope. When Jesus spoke of life he meant eternal life, which is something quite distinct from any idea of existence as we know it continuing for ever. Eternal life is fulness of life which begins, here and now, as a Christian comes, through belief in Christ, to be accepted by him through love for him. In its joy, in its wonder, it is a world away from the sad sheol of the Old Testament, the place of departed spirits. And though physical death is a stage along the path of life, for the Christian as for anyone else, it is only a stage. Death is absorbed by life. Indeed, the fulness of eternal life cannot be achieved without passing through death. What is mortal must be cast off, with all its limitations of time and decay, 'So that our mortal part may be absorbed into life immortal', as Paul puts it. (2 Cor 5.4).

In eternal life, indeed, 'We are in him who is real, since we are in his son Jesus Christ. This is the true God, this is eternal life', (John 5.20) a faith relationship with God through Christ. It offers hope of fulness of life with him, in the company of those whom we have loved and who have gone before us.

So the christian hope of the life of the world to come is a much more closely focussed concept than is any diffuse notion of a generalised, wish fulfilment inspired immortality for all. The christian hope is based upon a belief in a person, and upon an event which happened to that person - the resurrection of Jesus. And also it requires a response to that person, in belief and in service, before it becomes real. The background to this reality, the documentary evidence for it, is in the New Testament.

The Resurrection of Jesus.

The Gospels are focussed more on the death and resurrection of Jesus than upon anything else. All that goes before leads up to these tremendous happenings. The resurrection is the absolute heart and centre of the christian hope, not only of the life of the world to come, but of a christian hope of anything. 'If it is for this life only that Christ has given us hope, we of all men are most to be pitied. But the truth is Christ was raised to life'. (1 Cor 15.19).

Jesus died in the full physical sense. It was a dead man whose body was taken away for burial after the crucifixion. It was a living man, albeit clothed in a resurrection body, who returned first to astonish and then to overjoy his disciples. He had come through death. No one saw the happening. The actual resurrection is the great unseen event of the New Testament. It was also the great unexpected event. It was this, as Christopher Evans says, in *Resurrection and the New Testament,* 'which moved resurrection from the circumference to the centre of faith, and turned what was a matter of argument to a matter for joyful proclamation.' This, basically, is the good news of the Gospel from which flows so much else.

This good news became the centre of the Apostles' teaching from the earliest days of the faith. They knew it had happened. They believed as they came to ponder the mystery, that it was a fulfilment of Scriptural prophecy. But, above all, they found in it a dazzling hope of their own eternal destiny. Christ is in person the resurrection and the life. 'He who believes in me, though he die, yet, shall he live, and whoever lives and believes in me shall never die' (John 11.25). We will all 'rise' because Christ has risen. 'If the spirit of him who raised Jesus from the dead dwells in you, he who raised Jesus from the dead will give life to your mortal bodies also through his spirit which dwells in you (Romans 8.11).

The narratives of the resurrection appearances of Jesus give, as they are intended to, life and colour to those beliefs in the significance of what happened. 'Appearances' is not a very happy word, maybe, since it seems to suggest something insubstantial. The resurrection accounts, on the contrary, underline the concrete nature of these happenings. That marvellous story of how Mary Magdalen meets Jesus in the garden in the early morning does indeed suggest a strangeness about his physical self at that time: 'Do not hold me, for I have not yet ascended to the Father. . .' (John 20.17). But elsewhere the apostles see and touch him. On the road to Emmaus they do not recognise him by his appearance, although they talk with him at length. They recognise him by the manner in which, at the evening meal, he breaks bread, which was no doubt the point which the story was intended to make.

When these two disciples return from Emmaus to Jerusalem to report the happenings, another appearance follows which stresses the corporal reality of Jesus who 'stood among them. But they were startled and frightened, and supposed they saw a spirit. And he said to them: "Why are you troubled, and why do questions arise in your hearts? See my hands and my feet, that it is I myself; handle me and see; for a spirit has not flesh and bones as you see that I have." '. (Luke 24.36).

It is the same in the case of Thomas, the disciple

who is not prepared to accept any of this until he has actual physical contact with Jesus. 'Unless I see in his hands the print of the nails, and place my finger in the mark of the nails, and place my hand in his side, I will not believe'. (John 20.25). That is exactly what happened. Jesus does appear; Thomas does touch him, and is convinced with the words 'My Lord and my God!' he says.

Similarly, in a haunting tale of how, when a group of disciples are out fishing, much is made of the fact that they eat with him. It is at daybreak when they see a figure on the shore. When they land, having caught the fish which previously they had failed to do, they cook it and share it with him, not daring to ask who it is; but at the same time knowing it to be Jesus.

So the resurrection was real enough to those who met him and believed. They were chosen witnesses. Crowds saw him die; only a few saw him afterwards. Maybe there is an analogy here with the many to whom all this is nonsense, until they need it terribly, and the few to whom it is the word of life. Precious then is that word to those involved with the loss and sorrow which death brings. The answer to such loss and sorrow lies in the area of hope and trust; not of knowledge. What this hope and trust can mean in actual situations of everyday life and death we shall in a moment see. But first, there is one very specific statement of Jesus about the life of the world to come which rewards reverent examination, because it has meant so much to so many so often. 'Set your troubled hearts at rest. Trust in God always; trust also in me. There are many dwelling places in my Father's house; if it were not so I should have told you; for I am going there on purpose to prepare a place for you'. (John 14.1-2).

What did Jesus mean? Many have answered this is various ways. George McLeod found much illumination of this text in the fact that, in the ancient world, Caravanserais, staging points for caravans, were built to offer security to travellers when night fell. A messenger would customarily be sent ahead to prepare places. The picture sheds a small, homely light upon a great mystery.

There is one ever recurring question about death and what lies beyond. If the dead are indeed 'raised'; if people enter after death upon a new stage of being, what kind of body do they have? Christians in Corinth in the first century put that to Paul. For answer, he draws upon the analogy of the seed and that which grows from it. It has to die, he reminds them, before anything can come of it: 'What you sow is not the body which is to be, but a bare kernel, perhaps of wheat or of some other grain'. He is speaking of our physical body which, obviously, will at death perish. But then he goes on: 'What is sown is perishable, what is raised is imperishable. It is sown in dishonour. It is raised in glory. It is sown in weakness, it is raised in power, it is sown a physical body. It is raised a spiritual body'. (1 Cor. 15.42-44). And then he moves on to that terrific passage which echoes down the centuries, which has something to say about those people in those family photographs we were thinking of, wondering where they have all gone: 'When the perishable puts on the imperishable, and the mortal puts on immortality, then shall come to pass the saying that is written: "Death is swallowed up in victory. Oh death, where is they victory? Oh death, where is thy sting?" Thanks be to God who gives us the victory, through Our Lord Jesus Christ'.

This is what being 'saved' from death really means, and this is the essence of the New Testament message. The German theologian Eberhard Jungel, in *Death, the Riddle and the Mystery* sums it up: 'To be saved from death means to be set free for a new relationship to God and for a new relationship to one's self. This means that the threat which we ourselves imagine we must meet at the end of our lives has lost its power, that the curse of those actions which cause us to loose and forfeit our lives is broken. The death of Jesus Christ has set us free from the Law which in life and in death leaves us exposed to the nothingness of our actions (Romans 8.2). Salvation from death means therefore that we are set free both to live and to die. "If we live, we live to the Lord, and if we die, we die to the Lord; so then, whether we live or whether we die, we are the Lord's" '. (Romans 14.8).

The message for us
'We would not have you ignorant, brethren, con-

cerning those who are asleep, that you may not grieve as others do who have no hope'. (1 Thessalonians 4.13). Thus Paul wrote to the Christians in Thessalonica in the first century. What is it like to have 'no hope' in the twentieth? A very striking answer came in an article in *The Guardian* newspaper. The writer, in an honest and clearly deeply felt piece of investigative journalism, visited an undertakers' shop in a suburban high street. It was obviously the first time she had been in such a place. She had gone there, as part of an enquiry into funeral costs. What she found was something which moved her far beyond such mundane considerations. The place was staffed by husband and wife as a branch office of a large concern. They were called Dennis and Ada, and were very helpful, showing their visitor around. She, who had often wondered what such places were like 'felt the same guilty curiosity that children feel about sex — something it's not supposed to be nice to know'.

Yet it was all ordinary enough, with a Chapel of Rest, where coffins on trestles awaited collection. There was a visit from a customer, 'a sad weak woman' accompanied by a firm minded friend. The conversation which accompanied the filling in of the necessary forms was conducted almost in whispers. A clock on the wall could be heard ticking. Then all was done, and the customer, pausing at the door on the way out, spoke a little of her sadness. Ada said 'Yes . . . but you know what they say; "ours not to

31

reason why" ', upon which exit line the interview closed.

Still left, however, was the skilled observer who later wrote the article. She found herself progressively depressed. The details of the undertaking business — surely an essential service if ever there was one — were disturbing, maybe because so totally unfamiliar. She asked the woman who, with her husband, dealt so much in death, what her own views were. The reply was that she, who had had two coronaries, knew she could go at any minute, but was not afraid, and believed she would see the people she loved although she was not very religious. She said: 'When my mother died she was wrapped in a soft shawl, and I've still got it. Sometimes I put it on and wrap it round me and it smells lovely of her. You have to believe something, because it helps you'.

But the pay-off to this remarkable piece came in the concluding words of its writer: 'Nothing they said in the time I spent with them did anything to make me feel better about death. . . When it was nearly time to go Ada asked politely about my children and I found I couldn't bring myself to mention their names, or my husband's, for fear they'd take them down. When I left they said kindly and sincerely that they'd see me again, some day. But I couldn't suppress the thought that they meant feet towards the altar, in the Chapel of Rest'.

So there it all is — the modern version of 'no hope'. There, too, are all the characteristic accompanying features; revulsion, pity, fear. All are as old as the hills. Nor is belief in the christian hope going to remove the sorrow which is a necessary part of the life and death experience. What the christian hope does is to remove the hopelessness.

It is striking to move on from that to a scene depicting the fulness of christian hope in action. This came in a letter describing the death of a baby and what followed. The young parents had only recently become members of the Church in their commuter village. The narrator was the Vicar's wife who knew them well. 'The baby survived only four days after a last minute effort to save her. The parents now showed an admirable courage, insisting they wanted christian burial, saying if any Church friends wanted to come they would be glad. It was an occasion I shall never forget. Instead of natural sadness and grief being a matter for utterly private experience, it was shared, in a natural and spontaneous way by other young fathers and mothers of the Church family who came to be with them. The father carrying the little casket, accompanied the Rector from the cool church into the brilliant sun. As I looked around at the old tombstones, and at the group around the grave, the impression was of watching something timeless, as if the sorrows of all the centuries were gathered up inexplicably in that moment, as we stood where so many past generations had stood. Yet never, I think, could there have been more deep, basic and sincere feelings aroused in those present, as when the marvellous words of the christian faith: "I am the resurrection and the life" were awe-fully and yet triumphantly uttered. The other young fathers spontaneously stayed behind to fill in the grave'.

Such an account of such a happening, common-place and yet extra-ordinary, bridges the gap between New Testament times and the present, showing how the same hope animates both. What was said then is living in power now. It also demonstrates how a great deal of christian hope, including that of the life of the world to come, is experienced rather than intel-lectually comprehended. It is a gut reaction in the face of death to the word of life. And, of course, such an account as this moves everything a long way from that sad little office of the undertaker in the high street.

The pricelessness of the christian hope is never seen more clearly than in the bleakness of hopeless-ness, however fortified that may be by courage, or fled from by evasion. And its strength stands always in contrast to the powerlessness which death brings. There is nothing more helpless than a dead body. To touch the flaccid hand, to look upon the blank face from which all life has gone, is to be reminded how utterly dependant upon faith, unless we are prepared to accept this nothingness, is the hope which says resolutely that this is not by any means the whole story and that there is more to come. Michael Hollings sums it up in his book *The Shade of His Hand:* 'Much of life is touched with parting, in the very moment of our birth we part from our mother's womb. A number of people spend their lives trying to clamber back in, but most, however much they hate it, accept a continued measure of parting as inevitable all through life and into death. This is a true and wise and christian attitude. Let us admit we do not always manage to live it; but it is better for you and us and everyone if we face reality as Christ as man faced it. Life is for living and death is for dying, and we can say with the conviction of faith, resurrection is for all!'

For all? What happens to those who die believing none of these things or, more likely, knowing none of these things? A very large proportion in today's world are likely to be in this situation. Take the case of the husband of the woman, mentioned in the first sentence of this book who said, when he died; 'It's been such a shock'. He was, as it happened, a throughly good man: honest, patient, loving; in a modest way a very steadfast character. But religion in general, never mind the christian faith in particular, was simply not in his scheme of things, nor ever had been. Are we to say, therefore, that because of this he lies beyond the reach of God's mercy?

The Christian needs to be humble here, remembering that he is not a member of some privileged caste to whom alone, the love of God is offered. It may be that, through the grace of God, he has been enabled to know something of the hope that is in Jesus. In that case he has the possibility of sharing it with others, as opportunities and circumstances arise. But it is not for him, or for anyone else, to presume to judge even for a moment what the will of God is likely to be for this or that individual. The Bible has one great phrase never to be forgotten when the ultimate destiny of anybody is dwelt upon: 'The souls of the righteous are in the hands of God'. If God is God, and if God is loving, it can be held likely that the soul of that good and honest man who died so suddenly is indeed in his hands.

Nor may God's mercy extend only to the righteous. It may be his will that no one, however far from him in feeling, or however abandoned to the things of this world only, is ever beyond the reach of the wideness of his mercy. We cannot say. What we can do is avoid presuming to know what the divine will for anybody may ever be. Paul sums this up: 'The Gentiles do not have the Law; but whenever they do by instinct what the Law commands, they are their own Law, even though they do not have the Law. Their conduct shows that what the Law commands is written in their hearts. Their consciences also show that this is true, since their thoughts sometimes accuse them and sometimes defend them. And so, according to the good news I preach, this is how it will be on that day when God through Jesus Christ will judge the secret thoughts of all' (Romans 2.14-16. *Good News Bible*).

William Barclay says: 'I believe in the life to come, not because of the proofs of the philosophers, but because the whole teaching of the New Testament is based on the assumption that there is life after death'.

Thus fortified, and with the lights of faith and hope turned on, we can usefully now go on to look at some of the realities of that necessary preliminary to death — the experience of dying.

DYING

Christ leads us through no darker rooms
Than he went through before;
He that into God's Kingdom comes
Must enter by this door.

      Richard Baxter (1615-1691)

The Experience

Some of the fear associated with death is really fear
of dying. For the Christian, who can find truth in the
hope inherent in his faith it is a gateway to another
life. For the non-Christian, or for the unconvinced or
uncertain Christian, or for the dis-interested either
way, it is still a gateway, albeit with nothing expected
beyond it, and therefore, logically speaking, nothing
to experience, not even fear. But for all, dying itself is
an experience. It is a part of life, its closing chapter.
And since all life is of God, and comes from him, it
follows that death is likewise. It is thus a very proper
matter for the Christian to consider, being every bit
as God-given and God-ordained as life itself.

'It hath been often said that it is not death; but
dying, which is terrible', said the eighteenth century
writer Henry Fielding. But is it really terrible? It is
always a momentous happening; it is always at one
and the same time ordinary, as is birth, and extra-
ordinary, according as it is looked at from the viewpoint of the onlooker or the person involved. So

anybody's death is an unique event, in so far as they are involved; yet a commonplace event in so far as humanity in general is concerned.

That means that we are all concerned with it. Dying is not, therefore, something with which medical personnel only should be concerned. The illness associated with it is obviously their area. The care and companionship of the dying, however, reach beyond such circles. To leave it all to them, including all the spiritual, emotional, and practical issues involved, is not only unfair, but also a betrayal of the full humanity of those who are dying. What is more, it makes dying look like an illness which has gone wrong. Dying is not an illness which has gone wrong. It is the end of a life, and as such needs, so far as possible to be thought about as something distinct from the physical decay or malfunction which leads up to it.

Dying was once a communal matter, before urban living depersonalised life. It often took place at home, so that the departing person's family was around. Now the norm is for it to take place in hospital. And though this has great advantages, in the sense that many facilities are ready available to make the passage easier, it can still be a very lonely affair. It is not natural to die alone, although many do. A doctor speaking on a radio programme on this very subject recently told of a patient who 'having no one to die with', waited until a sympathetic sister came round, took her hand with the words 'I've been waiting for you', then promptly and peacefully died with his head on her breast. (B.B.C. Radio 4.2.5.77).

So dying, properly considered, is the concern of everyone in reach; relatives, friends, clergy or minister. To leave all to the medical people is quite possibly just another example of the modern idea that everything is in the end a technique best left to the experts involved, like plumbing to the plumber, or electrics to the electrician. But dying — the greatest 'do it yourself' venture that ever was, is just too big for that sort of treatment.

But is it 'terrible' as Fielding said? The word seems quite out of order. No one ought to generalise about the degree of suffering or non-suffering involved in dying. There are infinite varieties of experience in this matter. The psychiatrist, John Hinton, in his classic work on the subject, states, as a result of one hospital study, that it was found that whereas forty per cent of those under fifty experienced some suffering in dying, less than ten per cent of those over seventy did so. Perhaps this was why William Hunter, physician and anatomist, at the end of a long life, said on his death bed: 'if I had strength to hold a pen, I would write how easy and pleasant a thing it is to die'. But this is by no manner of means always the case, and should not be assumed to be so. Dying is too serious a matter for any false optimism; and to understate its gravity is to undersell its dignity. Everyone's dying is different. Any hospital can offer instances of dying brief, dying sudden, dying painful,

41

dying peaceful, dying distressed, dying unconscious. There is no norm to the experience.

Some fear of dying is innate and necessary, as a part of everyone's life-preserving instinct. If it were not so, life could too easily be thrown away, as indeed has sometimes been done by the abnormally and recklessly brave or by the emotionally disturbed. But fear of dying as a lonely venture into the unknown can be greatly alleviated by the companion-ship and support of those who, by previous thought about and around the subject have achieved sufficient self-adjustment to it to enable them to be a strength to those 'going up to the gate'. That is why it is so right for the Christian to endeavour to turn on as many lights of understanding as he can, in order to illuminate as much as possible of the area where this remarkable yet everyday happening takes place.

Some very interesting facts become visible. The first is the importance of an answer to the question as to when, in the process of dying, does death happen? An experienced general practitioner gave this answer: 'Definition of death has become confused rather than otherwise by recent developments. I have always thought the diagnosis of death at the moment it occurs, which one is always asked to do, is one of the more difficult decisions facing Doctors. Once a little time has elapsed the state is perfectly obvious to lay people as well. It looks as though it is useful now to consider brain death and physical death independent-ly. In christian terms I imagine brain death must be the primary consideration because the whereabouts of the spirit in the absence of an active brain must remain an enigma. Brain death can best be described as permanent loss of function of brain cells in the cerebral cortex so that all recognisable intellectual and mental activity ceases'.

The 'recent developments' to which he refers are life-supporting techniques which make it possible, in certain circumstances, for bodily functions such as respiration and blood circulation to be maintained even when brain function has apparently ceased. Instances of this in recent times have been the case of the brain-destroyed girl in the United States mechanically kept alive against the wishes of her parents, and the macabre life prolongation procedures adopted during the final illness of General Franco. Such possibilities raise sharp moral and ethical issues which, as this doctor says, confuse the question.

Meanwhile a working definition of death is that condition which is reached when all bodily and mental functions have ceased, and a definition of dying would be that it is the process, whether long or short, by which the state is reached.

Another interesting fact which emerges is that nobody standing on this side of the event knows what dying is like. The symptoms can be noted, and often have been. But the actual experience is a mystery. All we can note is what some people have said they expect dying to be like. There was a fascinating collection of these thoughts made for a radio feature a number of years ago.

'Leaving the physical body behind. It is a perfectly natural phenomenon. When God has finished with us on earth, we go to him'. 'A freedom of the spirit'. 'The gateway to another life, where I hope to meet my loved ones'. 'There is no feeling in death. I think you automatically sleep with the last thoughts you have in your mind, probably in the last hour or so of ordinary life. I think they stay with you until you wake up into the next world'.

Certainly there have been, to quote the doctor again, cases where 'prolonged coma with absent electroencephalogram activity has been followed by apparent total recovery.' In other words, there are cases where people appear to have died; but have in fact not done so. He adds: 'more frequently, cardiac arrest which will be followed inevitably by brain death in twenty minutes, is, if not corrected, a true physical death from which recovery is of course fairly frequent with current resuscitative techniques'. But such cases remain exceptional and, though the techniques used involve ethical problems, as we have said, they do not alter the fact that, when death has finally supervened, no one can describe the experience of 'going through the gate'.

One consequence of this is that, since observers of a dying person are always on the outside looking in, it follows that their judgements of what is happening can easily be affected by the fact that, being in full possession of their own faculties, they can assume a similar awareness in the dying person. The truth is often very different. Many people, though by no means all, drift off in a state of greatly lowered consciousness. A good deal of distress can be avoided if onlookers, such as relatives by the bedside, are gently reminded of that fact, including the truth that marked — sometimes even grotesque — changes of appearance and behaviour can take place without the patient necessarily knowing anything about it. The old phrase for dying, 'falling asleep' has often in it a grain of truth. It further follows from this that the time to make a helpful and caring relationship with the dying is before the final stage has been reached. The place of the very important last rites of the Church is another matter, and will be considered later.

And now, turning a few more lights on, let's look at some deaths as they have been said to happen, and to some others as they have in fact happened. John Betjeman's poem, *Death in Leamington* is a tender evocation of a familiar happening — the peaceful dying of an old person.

She died in an upstairs bedroom
By the light of the evening star
That shone through the plate glass window
From over Leamington Spa.

Beside her the lonely crochet
Lay patiently and unstirred,

But the fingers that would have worked it
Were dead as a spoken word. . .

Nurse looked at the silent bedstead
At the gray, decaying face,
As the calm of a Leamington evening
Drifted into the place.

She moved the table of bottles
Away from the bed to the wall;
And tiptoeing gently over the stairs
Turned down the gas in the hall.

It is not always like that. Here is a death which took place at home, and was in fact that of my own father, as recorded at the time. 'I reached the house at seven-thirty on a perfect summer evening. He knew me when I went in to him. The face was gray, the cheeks sunken. He took his hand from under the sheet and kissed mine. His breaths came and went, each a notable effort. He repeated after me the Twenty-third Psalm, The Lord's Prayer, The Nunc Dimittis, seeming to recognise each well known phrase with pleased and vehement recognition, as might one discovering a long overlooked import in a familiar thing. After that he seemed to drift away into unconsciousness. By eleven, the apparently inexhaustable daylight of June still lingering in the sky, his breaths came after longer and longer pauses. Then suddenly he breathed regularly about four times, then stopped. His watch, which had slipped out from under the pillow, said exactly eleven-ten'.

Such a commonplace dying, made memorable only because love and faith were present, is usual enough. There was certainly the sense that the dying man had passed the point of struggle, in so far as there was one, some time before, and that he had at the last no particular distress of which he was aware. This is corroborated strikingly in a letter to *The Times*, quoted by Norman Autton in his *Pastoral Care of The Dying*. The writer's father had died of a heart attack, following pneumonia, at the age of eighty-six. 'In the last stages there began the rapid laboured breathing which is a familiar feature of such cases. It was most distressing to hear and watch . . . the panting was so loud, so quick. However, my father being an exceptionally strong man, survived the dreadful night. In the morning his breathing became much quieter, he recovered consciousness, and said quite clearly 'tell the doctor I have had a very comfortable night'.

On the other hand, the event can be considerably more distressful in what might be called the 'run-up' to the final dissolution, and when the young are involved, much more so to those present as well. The same Doctor who spoke about the man who went 'promptly and peacefully with his head on the Sister's breast', mentioned also the case of a patient who was crying out in fear within an hour of her death.

Some of the death scenes of literature look artificial in the light of such realities. Did Oscar Wilde really utter a last witticism: 'one of us must go', referring to the vulgar wallpaper in his lodging? Did Keats really say: 'I feel the flowers growing over me'? Maybe Charles II's 'don't let poor Nelly starve' is nearer the mark, or the same monarch's apology to his waiting courtiers that he was 'an unconscionable time a-dying'. The account of the last days of Doctor Johnson, on the other hand, as carefully noted by Boswell, has a notable dignity and authenticity.

'Johnson . . . after being in much agitation, became quite composed, and continued so till his death. Previous to his receiving the Holy Sacrament in his apartment (he) composed and fervently uttered this prayer: "Almighty and most merciful Father I am now as to human eyes it seems about to commemorate for the last time the death of thy son, Jesus Christ, our Saviour and Redeemer. Grant, O Lord, that my whole hope and confidence may be in his merits, and thy mercy; enforce and accept my imperfect repentance: make this commemoration available to the confirmation of my faith, the establishment of my hope and the enlargement of my charity; and make the death of thy son Jesus Christ effectual to my redemption. Have mercy upon me, and pardon the multitude of my offences. Bless my friends; have mercy upon all men. Support me, by thy Holy Spirit, in the days of weakness, and at the hour of death; and receive me, at my death, to everlasting happiness, for the sake of Jesus Christ, Amen."

Having made his Will, and settled all his worldly affairs, he lingered till Monday, the thirteenth of that month, when he expired, about seven o'clock in the evening, with so little apparent pain that his attendants hardly perceived when his dissolution took place'.

Such an account suggests obviously that Johnson knew he was dying. But this is not always so, and the extent to which dying people are aware of it is open to question. Totally opposed answers have been given by medical personnel to enquiries made in the course of research for this book, ranging from 'never', through 'very rarely' to 'usually, although they don't like to talk about it'. Hinton in his book quotes two entirely opposed medical opinions. The first comes from Lord Horder: 'as for the dying man himself, we rarely find him "looking death in the eye", and knowing it is death. He is either very dubious that death is coming to him, or his appreciation is so dimmed, whether by weakness or by a merciful physician, that the end of life is a dream state rather than a true awareness'.

Yet another physician averred that 'most dying patients have the feeling that death is near. Some know it well enough and yet want nothing said about it; or perhaps, while they like to talk about it with Doctors and Nurses, they cannot bear to speak of it to their families. Obviously there is no norm, no fixed pattern of dying.

What difference does faith make?

The fixed point is the event itself. An important question to ask is how far, in observed practice, is religious faith relevant. John Hinton impartially looked at this question. Taking for purposes of study a group of hospital patients with terminal illnesses he found that, of those with any stated claim to religious belief, those who had firm religious faith and attended their Church weekly or frequently were most free of anxiety, only a fifth were apprehensive. He goes on to make a very thought-provoking statement: 'the next most confident group, in which only a quarter were anxious, were those who had frankly said they had practically no faith. The tepid believers, who professed faith but made little outward observance of it, were more anxious to a significant extent. They were twice as apprehensive as either the regular church-goers or those without religious faith. What part is played by religious belief in removing fear and how much by having a personality more able to adhere to convictions is hard to say. It was clear that for some people death was made acceptable in the context of their religious convictions'.

The short answer here, therefore, would seem to be that fear of dying comes more often — when it comes at all — to those who are uncertain about their beliefs, than to those who are christianly positive or agnostically negative. That is not to say that the last two attitudes are the same. To possess the christian hope is a priceless blessing. And though it is proper to admire the courage of those who can face dying without it but yet with equanimity, it is also difficult not to feel sorry when this is so. A life with all its strivings, and joys and sorrows, from the first cry of the new-born to the last breath of the dying, deserves a better close than nothingness. The christian hope gives that better end because it is animated by the conviction of a fresh beginning.

But there is more to be said on this in the way of direct reportage. The answers given by three people, a medical social worker, a clinical pharmacist whose work took him close to patients, and a vastly experienced nursing sister, each separately interviewed in a hospital, were more definite. Admittedly, all were themselves Christians: respectively Anglican, Baptist and Roman Catholic. But all were certainly professional enough to report things as they saw them, rather than as they thought they ought to be. The question put to each was: 'What difference does religious faith make to the dying?'

The Medical Social Worker, concerned with the personal and domestic problems of patients, said 'people who know that they are dying and accept it are often christian people who specifically voice the fact that they know they are dying. The staff on the ward always bring the clergy in on these things, and it is to them, I suppose, that they would chiefly talk. She said also that, apart from clergy: 'if it's a Christian friend ministering to a Christian it is very noticeable. You do recognise Christians. They often have

51

the Bible with them, and give their religion as something specific, like Methodist, Anglican, Catholic and so on. They are definitely comforted because they have another dimension. Any christian friend would obviously be a great comfort to them. But I just feel generally it has to be someone who has known them for a time, and who has built up a relationship'.

She did, however, find it necessary to add two things. The first was that some Christians were just as likely to delude themselves as to their condition as were others, such as the devout woman with cancer who, although she had nursed her mother and two aunts to their ends from a similar cause, quite refused to recognise the similarity in her own state. Secondly, she said that Christians were in a minority, and that the bitterness in some others, without that 'other dimension' was very striking and saddening. 'One of the things which shakes my faith as much as anything is to see the number of people who appear to drift out of this life still tormented by its problems. . . But I think that the people who have been good, stable persons in life, with happy family relationships or good relationships in the community, go out in the spirit. But many others seem to go out in anguish, which is said.'

Condensed and paraphrased, what she had to say on this point is really that, if you live in a mess, you are likely to die in one, also. The same point is made in another way by T.S. West, Deputy Director St. Christopher's Hospice, who, writing in the *Dictionary of Medical Ethics* says a man's 'ability to face the end of his life on this earth may spring from the manner in which that life has been led. Faith or courage or love do not often make their first appearance at the deathbed. However, if such virtues have at least been recognised during a man's lifetime it is often at the time of his dying that their reality and strength are revealed. All our lives we are preparing for death'.

The Clinical Pharmacist at the hospital where the Social Worker was interviewed said: 'the two people I know who have had a live christian faith have both been very serene and in fact their peace was noticed not only be fellow patients; but by members of staff, and even now one can speak about these people, and staff remember them. One in particular had a really marvellous peace and tranquillity, and knew exactly what was going on. His wife did, too, and together they were able to show a living christian faith. One contrasts this with people who do not have a faith, who appear to be very frightened. I am sure the Christian is also frightened; but not to the same extent, because he is able to depend upon the Lord for strength. Certainly I would say that a living faith does enable you to face up to death much more creatively'.

The Irish Ward Sister, whose whole life was lived very much at the sharp end, where people actually did their dying, said that faith made a very great difference indeed to the peace and resignation with which they could face things. But she did stress, as did her colleague the Medical Social Worker, that Christians were in a minority, and that some of them, too, fell short of the serenity and resolution which the faith enabled others to possess. An interesting point she added was that she felt the depersonalisation of the Health Service, together with the decline, as she felt it, of christian faith and practice in the world at large, were both contributory factors to a decline of its place in hospital life in general. Once, she recalled from the days of her training long ago, it was customary for a Nurse to kneel briefly by the dead; but now not so.

What kind of situation is being envisaged when the Christian encounters the dying? And who, to be still more specific, is the Christian envisaged? Let's take the questions in order. The situation envisaged is a very common one, where a relative or a friend or even someone chancily encountered at work or elsewhere, has become ill and values a visit. They may be in hospital, they may be at home. So the first need is to contact them and to try and build a bridge of understanding. It is needful to be prepared for rebuffs; but that is little enough to endure for Christ's sake. 'If when you do right and suffer for it, you take it patiently, you have God's approval'. (1 Peter 2.20).

It will sometimes be found, indeed, that the sharper the rebuff at the first stages of the encounter, the richer the relationship at the end of it. This is a strange thing. Here is an instance. Some parents had a dying child in hospital and I visited them, many years ago, as vicar of the parish. They were bitterly hostile. Life had wounded them. They were also lonely in a strange place, and the first person to come to them out of the cold had to receive the full venom of their despairing rage. Yet when it was over, and the poison drawn, there developed a most loving relationship until the child died, and indeed afterwards until they went their ways. It is good to know that they took something with them of the word of life and the enduring hope that somehow, somewhere, they would meet Micky — for that was the child's name — again.

And who is the Christian envisaged? It can be Priest, Minister, Layman or woman. The first two have their special duties. But all must start with friendship and loving concern. Doctor Collin Murray Parkes, in his book, *Bereavement; Studies of Grief in Adult Life,* makes the point that the role of the visiting Clergyman is similar to that of any other friendly person who wishes the bereaved well and would like to be of help. But what kind of help? That is the heart of the matter, more so with the dying, with whom we are here concerned, than with the bereaved. Friendship is much; but there is more to be given, once a relationship has been established with the dying person. The nature and creation of that relationship which is within the reach and legitimately within the concerns of any christian man or woman, clerical or lay, we shall consider later.

But first there is a vital matter to clarify. It is that

there is an analogy between sex instruction and what might be called death instruction. Both require self adjustment before they can be undertaken. The sad, painful, mutually embarrassing fidgetings and escapes into trivia which often accompany visits to the dying — a subtle undertaking at the best of times — are often due to the fact that such self adjustment has not been made. All concerned are on unfamiliar ground, at the very time when one of the parties must know where they stand. How, then, is such self adjustment to be attempted? It is by coming to terms with our own death first, before we can really have much to offer a dying person approaching theirs.

Besides this personal inner preparation, there are two other preliminary steps to be taken which can be most valuable in easing, and therefore in enriching, christian contacts with the dying. The first is the acquisition of some knowledge of what to expect, in the sense of how people die, what their emotional and physicial states are likely to be; and, secondly, how best in terms of a creative relationship they may be helped. All these matters arise out of the general matter of dying itself.

Self adjustment to dying
'And how if you were to die yourself?' asks Jeremy Taylor in *Holy Living and Holy Dying:* 'You know you must: only be ready for it by the preparations of a good life, and then it is the greatest good that ever happened to thee. Else there is nothing that can com-

fort you: but if you have served God in a holy life, send away the weepers; tell them it is as much intemperance to weep too much as to laugh too much: and when thou art alone, or with fitting company, die as thou shouldst, but do not die impatiently, and like a fox caught in a trap. For if you fear death, you shall never the more avoid it, and make it miserable'.

'The preparations of a good life. . .' That about sums up what, long before Jeremy Taylor, used to be called the *ars moriendi;* the art of dying. Its essence is how we live, as the Medical Social Worker put it, since living and dying are part of one whole. What it means to live as a Christian is of course a great matter in itself; 'with thankful remembrance of God's mercies, for his inestimable love in the redemption of the world by our Lord Jesus Christ; for the means of grace and for the hope of glory' at the heart of it. There are attitudes of mind, well within the reach of every man which makes the 'art of dying' a present reality. All three of them have been long tested by christian experience.

The first is to try and sit lightly to the things of this world. One reason is that we are creatures of the moment only, 'strangers and exiles on the earth' (Hebrews 11.13). Like people at an airport, we are passing through, and to imagine we are here to stay is to be as unreal as to imagine we can make a permanent home for ourselves in Heathrow. All we are really doing is waiting for our flight to be called. The more we can get this straight, the less difficult it will be when we move eventually into the departure lounge, and the more helpful we can be to fellow passengers who don't want to go.

William Law, in his *Serious Call to a Devout and Holy Life* has a marvellous description of a successful businessman caught by death at the very height of his career. Some neighbours visit him, looking suitably sad at the thought of a man in so promising a worldly state having to leave it all. To them he says: 'It is no trouble to me now to think that I am to die young, or before I have raised an estate. These things have now sunk into mere nothing. For if in a few days or hours I am to leave this carcass to be buried in the earth, and to find myself either for ever happy in the favour of God, or eternally separated from all light and peace, can any word sufficiently express the littleness of everything else? Is there any dream like the dream of life, which amuses us with neglect and disregard of these things?' And he then goes on, while yet there is time, to compose and prepare his soul.

The second attitude of mind important to the art of dying is to cultivate a preparedness for it. There is nothing morbid about this. What is morbid is a fearful avoidance of the subject. Yet, oddly enough, it was probably simpler in times past to achieve this mental adjustment. Death was so frequent a family visitor in victorian times, never mind in earlier centuries, that it was easy enough to be constantly reminded that 'in the midst of life we are in death'. But to be prepared for death is wise, because to be unprepared is to be vulnerable. And how can the Christian prepare? The answer can be given in two sentences. We need to practice dying by a daily exercise of self abandonment to the divine providence; only so may we approach it with confidence and our confidence is only in Jesus. We can trust him in death only in so far as we have learned to trust him in life.

So to sit lightly to the things of this world; and to be prepared for death by the practice of faith and trust in God and his purposes for us, are two of the three main elements in this art of dying. The third can be described in one word: acceptance. Not to exclaim against death; not to be surprised by the fact of it; but rather to live in the calm acceptance of the fact, the reality, and the necessity for it. And in proportion as we are able to achieve these attitudes, so we are likely to be able to offer help and comfort to the dying as opportunity serves.

Already we can have some idea of what to expect in the physical states of the terminally ill. As has been said, there is no norm, and therefore it is reasonable to expect a great variety of conditions. An important thing is not to be shocked or put off by any of them. Such resolution will not always, or even often, be required. But sometimes it will, and then, as always, it is a high duty to exercise it, so that the dying person may not receive from us any hint whatever of fear or revulsion. So it is important, and not particularly difficult, to expect, as regards physical states in the dying, pain sometimes, discomfort quite often, lethargy quite often, drowsiness, which can be drug induced, not uncommonly. In contrast, we can expect to find surprising alertness sometimes, accompanied by an understandable irritability arising out of boredom and immobility. These physical phenomena will obviously vary in relation to the stage the dying person has reached in their progress towards their bodily end. The great thing is to expect them as natural products of the situation.

But the emotional states to be encountered in the dying are more subtle matters, and differ from physical states in two important respects: they are not medical concerns solely; but rather belong to those who, in whatever capacity, can bring help and comfort. They also involve the total personality; not the body only. The similarity between physical and emotional states to be expected in those 'going up to the gate', is their variety. Anxiety and depression; loneliness, fear, perplexity and, most sadly, bitterness. This last can arise from a sense of failure and disappointment over what has happened, or rather not happened, in the life which is closing down. I can recall a man, who almost to the end, dwelt morosely upon the fact that he had never been made a director of a long forgotten company for which he had once worked.

But bitterness can come from more sombre sources — a sense of betrayal by those who should have been loving. Sadly, this seems increasingly prevalent as social and economic circumstances change. The

Medical Social Worker already quoted said on this matter: 'these days one problem with a lot of people who are dying is that most of the family, including the womenfolk, are working, and family finances are based on this income. It's very difficult for the woman just to be able to drop her job, especially when she knows that her husband is going to be dead in, say a couple of months, and that she will need that job to fall back on financially and emotionally. What a dying person really needs is to be able to go home, and for someone whom they love to look after them, whenever possible.'

Speaking of cancer patients in particular she said: 'with this sort of disease men who get it have often been ill over a long period and their wives may have gone somewhere else for comfort. This happens nowadays quite often, and we get these men who know this, and know that their wives don't bother to visit them much and they are very bitter. We've known people get a solicitor in at the very last minute trying to cut their wives off from money or children, and, bitter to the end, they go out. It is very sad'. It is indeed; but it is part of the hard face which the world as it is can show even to the dying. How then can they be helped?

Helping the dying

The term 'helping' here has a wide connotation. For the Christian it can mean anything from the slow building up of a concerned relationship, to the actual speaking about spiritual things. That last stage may never be reached, except by the Priest or Minister and sometimes not by them. Any sort or manner of what might be called religious aggressiveness is to be avoided. The Sister already quoted had a horrific story of the disturbance caused in her Ward by a zealot who exhorted a young man, who had no idea he was dying, to prepare for his end. The patient was terrified, the relative enraged, and the Sister herself reprimanded for letting the zealot in! But even when there is no opportunity of direct mention of spiritual matters a good work for God has been done when love has been shown, companionship offered and, perhaps above all else, a willingness to listen made plain, once a mutual trust has been established.

An anxious person can be enormously helped by being encouraged to talk about his anxieties. This is one place where the blessed capacity to listen can prove its worth. Any visitor, relative, friend or Minister is richly rewarded when, as he rises to go, the sick person may say; 'I feel better for our talk', even though the visitor has in fact said very little.

But the anxieties of the gravely ill should never be underrated. They are far more than a mood. They often have very solid bases, such as what is going to happen, will the pain return, and so on. And there are quite common conditions such as breathlessness which can make a sick person very anxious indeed. This is where supportive companionship, perhaps based upon a regularity of visiting, can be of priceless value. Visits are badly needed and yet are often lacking. The dying, in an age of little faith, seem to arouse fear and encourage withdrawal from them.

This in its turn can accentuate depression. And here again there can often be deeper causes, including an elemental sorrow at loosing all that life has to give.

The hope of another life with more to give can mean much here, always provided that a life time of indifference has not blinded the eyes and clouded the understanding to such an extent that even the very notion of it is, but for the grace of God, meaningless. Failure of physical powers, especially in those who have been strong and self reliant, can be very depressing indeed, as can be concern for those who are going to be left.

The loneliness of the dying can be very marked, for reasons already given. Archbishop Anthony Bloom, quoted by Norman Autton, once said to a conference of hospital chaplains: 'One of the tragic things I find in the West is the gradual loneliness in which a dying person is secluded. The person knows, in body and soul, that death is coming; but the husband smiles, the daughter smiles, the nurse smiles, the doctor smiles, everyone smiles in such a way that the person knows it is a lie . . . and the result is distress, to be faced in a lonely way . . .' A patient's poem, originally printed in *The Nursing Mirror,* and quoted by Doctor R.G. Twycross, Research Fellow at St.

Christopher's Hospice, in his book *The Dying Patient*,
makes this point powerfully:

I huddle warm inside my corner bed,
Watching the other patients sipping tea.
I wonder why I'm so long getting well,
And why it is no one will talk to me.

The nurses are so kind. They brush my hair
On days I feel too ill to read or sew.
I smile and chat, try not to show my fear,
They cannot tell me what I want to know.

The visitors come in. I see their eyes
Become embarrassed as they pass my bed.
'What lovely flowers' they say, then hurry on
In case their faces show what can't be said.

The Chaplain passes on his weekly round
With friendly smile and calm, untroubled brow.
He speaks with deep sincerity of life.
I'd like to speak of death, but don't know how.

The surgeon comes, with student retinue,
Mutters to sister, deaf to my silent plea.
I want to tell this dread I feel inside,
But they are all too kind to talk to me.

Here again the homely and deeply christian act of
giving time can be of very great value, always

remembering that security and companionship are, as Autton points out, primary needs of the dying. The same truth applies also to the emotional states of fear and perplexity. Contact must be made and a relationship established before anything meaningful can be done or said. Even then, perhaps the most important truth of all is that it is often not what the visitor does or says which matters so much as what kind of a person he or she is. If they can carry with them the infection of faith and courage and personal adjustment to the fact of death, then they have introduced to the bedside about the only really beneficial infection there is.

There is a powerful prayer in Michael Holling's *The Shade of His Hand,* which expresses something of the courage which can be required even by the visitor: 'She wrote and told me she had cancer and not to be shocked when I saw her. But Lord, I never guessed. When I saw her two years ago she was a fine, strong woman, beautiful. Now, Lord, she is a bag of bones, her hands like birds' claws, her face shrunken in, her eyes burning with fever. Of God, it hurts to see her pain, her struggle to breathe. And Lord, the memory hurts — that she will not walk again, or come out into the garden she loved, or visit the poor, or go to church. It hurts, yet she is still alive, alert, thoughtful, loving, and somehow that makes it hurt more. Help me to help her in love'.

But not all is sorrow and pain. There can often be found an entry point to a meaningful relationship through familiar things of everyday. Part of the solitariness of the dying is that they feel out of things. A man likes to hear about how things are coming along in his garden even if he is unlikely to see it again. A woman will love to hear of the family, and of other people's, all the more so when she is to part from them, as regards this world, for ever. Such matters are dear, and human, and talk of them is truly christian. It can also lead, by stages, from the known to the unknown, so that a talk on gardens may pass eventually to the hope of that ultimate and most beautiful of gardens where the flowers are eternal.

There is also a down to earth issue which can trouble sick people, especially the old, who will show their anxiety by returning to it over and over again. This is the question as to whether they have 'put their affairs in order'. When this matter is mentioned it is quite often one of the first indications that they have some inkling of their true condition. For a friend or relative or clergyman to follow this up can be 'a very present help in trouble', particularly to a troubled mind. It is, in fact, one of the things which the Prayer Book Office for the Visitation of The Sick specifically suggests should be done. So it is helpful to be able to give advice. And such odd pieces of knowledge as, for instance, how to go about making a Will, can be most useful.

The Christian has also, in relation to the dying as to anyone else, a ministry of reconciliation. A deathbed above all is the wrong place upon which to nurse resentments and bitternesses. Therefore to help people to overcome them, by pointing to the better way of forgiveness, is to do well for God. Not for nothing does that same Prayer Book Office — a too often neglected repository of wisdom — require of the Minister to ask of the sick person whether he 'be in charity with all the world'. He is also to ask him 'to forgive, from the bottom of his heart, all persons that have offended him.' By the same token, 'if he hath offended any other' he is to ask them forgiveness. And where he has 'done injury or wrong to any man', he is to be persuaded to 'make amends to the uttermost of his power'.

Obviously, people do not talk like that any more. But they do talk about those very same things. Nothing really changes, age after age, in this area. And even if someone has never given a thought to God, he may yet want to make such gestures as these at the end. And if so, he should be encouraged to do so.

To speak directly of the christian hope requires great tact. Sometimes a layman or woman can do this most effectively. The Clinical Pharmacist already quoted was one who himself did this, although with much circumspection. He said: 'One always goes about it in a round about way. Some patients have Bibles by their side. So one can ask if they have used it. I say "I read the Bible, and in many circumstances I find it helpful, particularly when I've gone through crises. I have found that praying helps too. Have you considered this?" One takes it from there. When I go to speak to people on these lines I try to feel led by the Holy Spirit, so I would try always to ensure, as far as I can, that it is the will of God for me to speak on these lines to some particular person, and in the majority of cases I have found them receptive. Sometimes there's a rebuff; but I still think you have to try try and help in a friendly way'. The modesty of this account was counterbalanced by the testimony given unasked by some other members of staff to the good done by this man.

The difficulty of getting through to the dying with a specifically christian message is obliquely made plain by a remark of C.S. Lewis in *The Problem of Pain:* 'It is safe to tell the pure in heart that they shall see God, for only the pure in heart want to'. That obviously leaves a lot of people out: the unsure, the unprepared, the indifferent. The difficulty thus presented bears particularly on clergy and ministers who, by virtue of office, are expected to have specific things to say and do. Norman Autton quotes Kurt Eissler as saying, in his book *The Psychiatrist and the Dying Patient:* 'The priest or minister is in a more favourable position (than is the psychiatrist) since he is a representative of the power beyond, before which the faithful who is dying believes he will soon appear'.

It is a surprising opinion. As with Autton himself, who says 'this may be so', many clergy would want to question it. In hard fact, the task of clergy in ministering to the dying, especially in so secularised a world as ours, is both difficult and delicate, because so often there is no infrastructure of belief to build upon. When there is, then obviously the position is much clearer, and the priest's ministry can be, to use Autton's phrase, 'direct and devotional . . . the priest will encourage the dying patient to lean on his faith and the faith of the whole Church, and assure him that he is being surrounded by love and prayer'. He may bring the last Sacraments, especially of Holy Communion. This, as also the Sacrament of Holy Unction, when it is used, presents opportunities for involving the family and having them present at a memorable time. Indeed, the care of the family, especially husband or wife of the dying person, can be as important an aspect of the priest's or minister's work at such a time as anything else.

But, as with the manner of dying itself, there is no norm as to what clergy may find themselves able to do, or not to do. If ever there was a case of 'playing it by ear' this is one. And, the coin which bears on one side the image of the clergyman as an alarming apparition associated with frightening hints of impending death, carries on the other that of a kindly presence who can do much, even more than he always realises, to ease the passage from this world. The dying person may well look to the doctor for a cure. When it is not to be had, he can still look to the priest for hope.

And often, in the giving of that hope, the simplest

things suffice: the holding of a hand, the murmuring of a prayer: above·all the giving of time. Anthony Bloom, again as quoted by Autton, has said that 'simply being with the dying, hours together, saying nothing: this is an ability which I dare say clergy should develop, the ability to sit with someone, saying or doing nothing. . . Just to sit and go deep . . . showing that your presence speaks; that if there is a need, you can put your hand on the person and it will mean more than whatever you can say'.

Let a simple story illustrate this. Visiting at a hospital, I passed a bed screened round. A glimpse within showed a middle aged man obviously dying and entirely alone. I went in, and for a very long time, held his hand. To this day the memory of that big, heavy hand survives, as also does the sound of the radio coming tinnily from the disregarded headphones hanging askew on the bedhead. Eventually he died. Who was he? I never knew, other than that he was a man and a brother and that it was good to be with him. And as for those who die without wanting at all any prayers at any time with any clergyman, let him remember that it is his privilege to offer prayers *for* them, that they may go on their way not entirely alone to what they may think is the dark.

But there is another kind of dying quite different from any mentioned so far. This is the long term, slow motion dying, frequently of the elderly. It is increasingly common as medical techniques enable people to live longer — sometimes too long — and often causes severe stress on all concerned. There is a challenging opportunity for christian service here, not only to the dying; but to those who have charge of them. Who has not witnessed families in which the prolonged caring for an elderly relative has produced truly appalling stresses? Nor are such situations always caused by age. They can also happen with the slowly degenerative diseases which can make equally severe demands upon all concerned. Such states can be truly described as dying. The only difference between them and the customary deathbed is one of tempo. But today's overflowing geriatric hospitals — a wry tribute to medical progress — can lead to experiences of dying scarcely recognised in the deathbed literature of the past, where the process was generally expected to be brief, and the desirable accompaniments of it, in christian terms, were seen to be repentance, acceptance, peace, and then departure.

Such a sequence is scarcely possible with the slow motion dying which, like a slowed down film, makes the action seem longer than it ought to be, or desirably should. The Senior Nursing Officer of a famous hospital, speaking at a conference on 'Living with Death', made the good point that 'concentration on how to keep alive weakens the ability to die'. Certainly, an unthinking acceptance of the principle of life — prolongation at any price-has let to serious ethical problems which have yet to be thought through.

What can be a specifically christian contribution to

such situations? Two facts are clear; that there is the time, often lacking in other cases, for the building up of a close relationship with the person afflicted and with relatives, and that there is opportunity, through personal service, to ease the load carried by those bearing too much. There could well be an opportunity here for the sick-room equivalent of baby sitting, whereby the visitor can make it possible for the usually housebound relative to have time off.

In such circumstances there is also the expectation of being able to speak at leisure, and as opportunity serves, never forcing the issue or unnaturally introducing it, of the christian hope, the love of God, and the companionship of Christ, here and hereafter. Regular visits, each as far as possible with a clear purpose, such as the sharing of a common interest, from general news to a game of chess, can sometimes form a down to earth platform upon which, later, a modest ladder to heaven may be set up. Someone who has, over a period of time, talked about, say, gardening, will find it easier eventually to talk about God.

Such christian service can often bring with it a reward for the giver none the less rich for being unsought. The courage of the slowly dying in some instances is so inspiring that it is a privilege to encounter it. There is, for instance, — for she is still living, if her existence can be so described — a woman whom a severe stroke laid low after a singularly active and productive life. Paralysis resulting, with incontinence and other humiliating conditions, she has been sent to a hospital bed where, like a long term prisoner she still is. But, being of an unconquerable spirit, she wrote, in a letter to her friends, her thoughts upon this severe sentence in such terms as to uplift the hearts of those who read it.

'For more than a year now I've been trying, often desperately, to sort out this jigsaw muddle of strokes and bedwetting — what's the most worthwhile way to cope with it all, and not waste the chance of a lifetime to move and live in spite, in fact because of, all this fear and unsteadiness which often sweep over me and nearly drown me. So much of it is what, before, I'd have thought I could cope with but now find I cannot. And at night, lying awake with pain in my leg, and the noise in the ward, I keep peeling off skins to get down to what, in actual fact, does get me through the next dreaded night and equally dreaded day. I go over and over parts of Psalm 73 and now I know the writer must also have had a thrombosis and a stroke. In one of the modern translations it goes like this: "When my heart had been growing bitter with pains shooting through my loins, I simply failed to understand my attitude to you was brutish. Even so I stayed in your presence. You held my right hand. . ." I try to hold on to those words of Mother Julian's: 'All shall be well, and all manner of things shall be well".

In some nights of misery I find I'm just stupidly refusing to say them because so much of me says I don't believe it. I find I get disproportionately annoyed about things like incessant noise — radio on every moment and television on non stop. . . "but be with him" — Mother Julian of Norwich again. But it means nothing unless when we say it we mean something about bedpans and entire crippled dependence on a nurse taking us to the toilet. Bladder and bowels must take their essential place in "O all ye works of the Lord, bless ye the Lord". You are loved. Where does that come from? You are loved. In that lies the truth of your life. That love comes through a multitude of streams and brooks now hidden, now seen, now lost to sight. All inadequate but running together till the great ocean of his love is reached. My brook became a river, and my river became a sea'.

To encounter such bed-rock truth, such suffering so near to the Cross is some of the reward which can come from contacts with the dying. Equally, such contacts can bring anguish and a testing of faith, especially when physical suffering is involved. This part of the picture, has been lightened to some degree in recent years by the recognition that care of the dying is an art in itself, involving psychological, social, pastoral and medical care working together to achieve, as far as may be, a good dying.

The pioneer work of Doctor Cicely Saunders and her Staff at St Christopher's Hospice, Sydenham, has done much to revive in a modern form the *ars moriendi,* or art of dying. The control of pain through skilled use of drugs has been a blessed development. Fortunately St Christopher's is not alone in this field. There now exist specialist centres in various parts of the country where terminally ill patients are nursed to the end. The National Society for Cancer Relief has seven 'continuing care units'; the Marie Curie Foundation has eleven. Others are maintained by independent charities or religious orders. Here is how one of these felt and looked when visited.

It lay up a winding drive among woods. Medically, it was totally professional. Spiritually, the impression was of great, though unobtrusive power. The terminally ill were here part of a greater whole, so that patients came and went and were treated elsewhere in the place as in any general hospital. It was only in what they called the 'Special Care Wards' that those who were, knowingly or unknowingly, 'going up to the gate' were to be found.

Here, it seemed, was a concentration in actuality of all the problems and the gropings, the hopings and the mysteries, the sufferings and the joys, which forever surround the experience of dying. And here, too, oddly enough, were answers to some of the questions which arise. The mysterious fact was that the answers, like the questions, seemed so much simpler when they were encountered in this deeply christian atmosphere. Those problems of whether the dying were aware of their condition, for instance, and whether they should be told, here looked entirely different because there seemed, in the minds of the staff, no such category as 'the dying'. They did not recognise categories, or, apparently, any theoretical questions whatsoever. All they knew about or cared about, as far as it was possible to ascertain, were the people in their charge. And everyone of those was different, as no doubt to Christ everyone is different, too.

There was, for example, a woman whom we may call Constance. Thirty, married, two children, aged six and four. Their visits were a joy. There were always presents for them from staff, and they would run about the corridors while the father spoke with his wife. She did know of her condition, having been told by her doctor at her own request before her arrival. This had enabled her to share the knowledge with her husband and so to enable him to achieve some acceptance of the situation. She lay, semi-conscious on the autumn morning, looking out at the wind-swayed trees beyond the window.

And then there was Arthur, a hefty middle aged man in good spirits, convinced that his physiotherapy treatment, from which he had just returned, was doing him good. He also was terminally ill, without having the slightest inkling of the fact. Nor would he ever have, for to tell him would be to destroy him utterly. It was quite different with Jim. He knew and had, in a strange way, been greatly relieved by the information. Progressively becoming slow and weak, he had been equally progressively unable to keep up with his work. For this he had blamed himself, imputing it to some inexplicable weakness of character.

Now suddenly all was clear. There was no blame to be borne. It was not his fault, after all. And that, it seemed, was a wonderful and releasing thing to know.

And then again there was the grotesquely deformed and convoluted Anglican Priest whose energetic life, at home and overseas, had come to this. It was impossible to tell whether he was reachable by speech. To the lay eye he looked distressed. Matron — they still used the old title here — said, however, that he was not suffering in any way.

And what about that question of how far it was desirable, and how often possible, to speak directly of spiritual matters? In this place it did not seem to arise. It did not appear even to be understood, as a question. It was just done on a modest scale. Such phrases from staff as 'I'll say a little prayer for you', came naturally, and were so taken. 'We put up a barrier', Matron said, 'in asking who is christian and who isn't: who would want us to pray for them, and who wouldn't. There is no need for that. Prayer reaches through. We shouldn't put up barriers, ever. Anyway, very few people really and truly at the end are indifferent to such things'. This place held some endearing characteristics. One was the habit of sticking up inspirational notices here and there on doors. One was 'Theme of the Week: keep me going, Lord'. Another, super-imposed upon a seascape, read: 'When the tide is at the ebb, full tide is on the way in'.

But, whatever is done, whatever happens, it remains true that dying, the natural concommitant of being born is a 'do it yourself' affair, surrounded by many mysteries never to be solved in this world.

There must come a time when, to use a memorable phrase of the Ward Sister quoted earlier, all that remains is 'tender loving care'. It is time now, therefore, to turn a light upon that which follows — death itself.

DEATH

We are happier with death than we should ever have been without it.

Sir Thomas Browne: *Religio Medici*

Timely death
They were born with a red circular spot on the forehead, directly over the left eyebrow. In the course of time the mark grew larger, gradually changing colour until it was coal black, never altering there-after or forever, because those bearing it could never die. These were the Struldbugs, described in one of Swift's lesser known parts of Gulliver's Travels, as a unique kind of men and women who appeared occasionally in the country he was visiting.

When told of them Gulliver at first imagined them to be particularly fortunate beings. Since death could never take them, they would have endless time in which to become wise and rich. And their passing could never bring sorrow to those who loved them because they would have no passing. But the natives of the country soon corrected him. The birth of a Struldbug was always a cause of universal lamentation. Their endless life was a misery. As their own generation died, they were left isolated among strangers, as in an eternal geriatric ward.

Even a non-eternal geriatric ward can be sad enough, and the problems created by the old they cater for make this Struldbug story strangely contemporary. 'Outside are the minibuses and the ambulances', said a writer describing one recently, 'inside is oblivion. Thirty very aged people, almost all women, are sitting side by side, immobile around the walls of a large room. Their heads don't turn, and their eyes don't move at any sound or movement . . . Some slump, head on chest, eyes open. Some are upright. All stare mutely at the walls and windows opposite. For hours and hours a radio plays subliminal muzak. Two budgies caged in the centre of the room twitter. Here the old sit; weeks, months, years . . .' *Guardian* 17.11.77.

So for the Struldbugs endless life became intolerable. Everywhere else, Gulliver was told, long life may be the universal desire and wish of mankind. But with them it was not so: 'The appetite for living was not so eager, from the continual example of the Struldbugs before their eyes'.

It is a powerful parable with an important message: that a recognition of the necessity of death is just as vital as acceptance of the fact of it. Death can indeed be truly welcome and blessed. The point was well made in a radio discussion on *Attitudes to Death* recently when one of the speakers pointed out that once the necessity of it had been recognised it was possible to cease thinking of it as some kind of calamity or failure. Jeremy Taylor puts it well: 'It is no more than a man does every day: for every night death hath gotten possession of that day, and we shall never live that day over again. . . And what is sleeping and waking, but living and dying? What is Spring and Autumn, youth and old age, morning and evening, but real images of life and death?' And of the dead he says: 'Since we hope he has gone to God, it is an ill expression of our love to them that we weep: for that life is not best which is longest, and it shall not be enquired how long they have lived; but how well'.

Death seen in this way, with some light of understanding turned on, looks very different from the apparition of darkened imaginings which it too often is. That is not to say that death can be shrugged off. But seen as a necessity it does indeed appear as a far more acceptable part of the total human experience. Already there are some indications that this is becoming gradually recognised. The *Chicago Daily News*, to take an example of frankness not yet equalled here, has run a twice a month column under the title *A Time To Live*, concerned actually with the remaining part of that quotation, 'and a time to die', and written for those under the shadow of death, either their own or someone else's. The writer, Jory Graham, herself with terminal cancer, had the excellent idea of creating this column in order to share her experience with others. But this is an exception, and there is a long way yet to go before death comes generally to be seen for what it is — a necessity, in the fullness of time.

Untimely death

It is when it is not in the fullness of time, when it is not the proper conclusion to a long life, that severe problems arise. For the Christian, who believes in a God of love, and part of whose witness is to justify the ways of God to man, the deaths of children and young people are likely to be especially challenging. There is a great distinction between tragic death, such as that of the young mother mentioned earlier, and the often welcome passing of the elderly. Maybe that is why most of the many comforting words which have been written about it are concerned with timely rather than untimely deaths. It is much easier to be philosophic about death which comes as a release, than when it bears all the marks of a tragedy. This remains a dark area. Sometimes, indeed, it can be especially dark to those whose strong faith in God's love and care is put to severe test by some apparently meaningless loss. We need to come to terms, as far as may be, with this mystery, always remembering that we are not likely to be able to be of much comfort to others, let alone to ourselves, until we do.

We are back now to the question asked in the pro-logue to this book: 'What should be, what could be, the christian message to the parents of a son written off in a motorway fog pile up?'

There is a message to be given, and a high and hopeful one. What needs to be understood is that it is constantly under test, and has often to survive in highly hostile environments, as when people are embittered by grief, and the old, old but ever new questions come tumbling out: 'Why did God allow this to happen?' 'Shall we meet again?' The message and the answers are to be found in the christian hope of the life of the world to come, based on a living faith in Christ. Our concern now is with how that faith survives when people are stricken by grief and baffled by some apparently pointless tragedy which has befallen them.

Here is an actual instance. The much loved daughter of ardently christian parents died, at the age of twenty-three, from a brain tumour. So unexpected was the final onset that the event happened when parents and daughter were abroad on holiday. She actually died in a hotel bedroom in a strange land. The girl had fully shared her parents' faith, and had indeed chosen the nursing of sick children as her way of expressing it in action. And yet she died, distressingly and in distress. Why had God allowed this to happen?

The question appeared to press especially hard on her father, a man who, in his combination of prosperity and good deeds, resembled Job, a 'man blameless and upright, one who feared God and turned away from evil'. It was in fact this Book of Job to which he turned for some light in his darkness. There was the archetypal man of God upon whom blow after blow fell, taking eventually all that he had: his possessions, his family, then even his own health. From the depths of his sufferings Job asked, just as did this father: 'Why is light given to him that is in misery, and life to the bitter in soul?' (Job 3.20).

That is the constantly recurring question age after age. But this bereaved father found one passage in particular which calmed his soul even if it did not explain his daughter's death. It is when Job finally acknowledges that the mystery of his sufferings is too big for him; but not too big for God. 'I know that thou canst do all things, and that no purpose of thine can be thwarted'. (Job 42.2) What can make untimely death unendurable is when no purpose in it whatever can be felt. But here was a passage saying that God has a purpose, in all and through all, but that it is far beyond our limited human capacity to understand.

But that is, in a sense, negative comfort. More positive is the Cross, which is the great sign and surety of God's mercy in the face of death at its harshest. 'For God so loved the world that he gave his only son, that whoever believes in him should not perish but have eternal life'. (John 3.16). A God who cares to that degree is not one to abandon us in our sorrows. We may look with confidence to him to show us a way through. That in fact is what happened to this shattered father. He was shown how to pick up the fragments of his life, piece by piece. After incredulity that such a thing could happen to him came a feeling of guilt, as if he had himself failed his child. Then came anger towards God, equally point-less. Then a feeling that things could never be the same again, and after that the revelation that this was in fact true. Things could never be the same again. Acceptance of it saved the day, together with the recognition of the fact that a new life offered new opportunities of service. From that point onwards his sorrow became creative, instead of the continuing bitterness which untimely death can bring.

The Cross is the sign also that God in Christ is himself to be found in this valley of the shadow. 'He was despised and rejected by men; a man of sorrows and acquainted with grief . . . surely he has borne our griefs and carried our sorrows. . .' (Isaiah 53.3-4). The significance of what many have seen as a prophetic description of the Christ to come is not only that he has borne our griefs; but does do so here and now continually. God has never promised that we shall not pass through deep waters; but that he will be with us when we do. The world is a dangerous place. Untimely death, by disease or accidents, will happen so long as we are in it. They are part of the consequences of living. We give hostages to fortune every time we bring children into the world. 'Time and chance happens to them all' said the wise old writer of Ecclesiastes. And just because living is dangerous, life is an adventure, constantly fraught with the consequences of triumph or disaster. For the same reason courage is necessary, and faith all the more precious.

It is much to know that Christ is there with us in our valley of the shadow, because he is also able to lead us out of it into the light. That priest and poet now undeservedly forgotten, Geoffrey Studdert Kennedy, put this well in a poem he called *The Suffering God:*

'Father, if he, the Christ, were thy revealer,
Truly the first begotten of the Lord,
Then must thou be a sufferer and a healer
Pierced to the heart by the sorrow of the sword.

Then must it mean, not only that thy sorrow
Smote thee that once upon the lonely tree,
But that today, tonight and on the morrow
Still it will come, O gallant God, to thee.'

He ends with a fine message to all wandering in this dark area of untimely death:

'Give me, for light, the sunshine of thy sorrow,
Give me, for shelter, shadow of thy cross.
Give me to share the glory of thy morrow,
Gone from my heart the bitterness of loss.'

That bitterness of loss was experienced by the parents of a small girl run down by a lorry and killed at the beginning of the summer holidays of a year or so ago. The vicar of the parish, in his monthly letter to his people, wrote very strikingly upon this event, which had saddened the whole community. What he said combines the wisdom of Job's acceptance of charity with the hope and mercy to be found in the love of Christ. 'The Christian may well be shocked by sudden death, especially of children. This is more particularly the case in our time, when we can assume that it is normal for people to grow up and experience some fulness of life on earth. But the deeper questions which may face us are to do with the love of God. Can we accept the shallow, crude assumption of the world around us that there is a sort of standard length of earthly life that everyone should expect, and if they do not get it there is something wrong?

The family into which I myself was born had two members who died before they were two years old, One at the age of four, another carried off by a road accident at thirty-nine, and parents who lived to seventy-nine and ninety four. There is something very wrong with that pattern if you suppose that God's love must be displayed by some standard length of years. For myself, as a Christian, I believe that God's love and care is as great for my brothers and sisters, who had so short a time, as it is for my parents whose years were unusually long.

'If that belief is to make sense, it has to be buttressed by two others. One can be found in the Old Testament, and demands both humility and awe before the greatness of God. It is best expressed in the words of Job who, in the face of complete castatrophe falling on his family, says, "The Lord gave, and the Lord has taken away; blessed be the name of the Lord". Something much less stark and more tolerable to us who lack the courage and submission of Job is vouchsafed by the Heavenly Father through Jesus; it is the promise of risen and eternal life with him in his Kingdom of love.

'It seems a tragedy to me that so many Christians in our time seem to find it hard to accept this integral part of the christian faith. Is it because this material and half rational experience of our daily life in this world gives such entire fulfilment of human hopes that nothing more seems necessary? If you think that, you are surely denying God's boundless love to the many millions whose lives in this world are short, stunted, handicapped, or miserable in any number of ways. The promise of the Gospel, 'Give light to them that sit in darkness and in the shadow of death," seems to me to be dust and ashes to millions if we leave out the promise of eternal life.'

The faith that God's loving care keeps those who go trustfully through the gate of death, and that the crucified Jesus is present with those who bear the burden of sorrow, can and does bring light and healing to broken spirits.

One question remains: 'Shall we meet again and know each other after death'. It could well be asked by the parents of that child killed by the lorry, or by the husband of Constance, the young wife who has by now gone from him; and by the father of the young nurse who died, and by anybody at any time struck down in this way. William Barclay was himself

one of them, for he lost a young daughter in a drown-
ing accident. That fact gives him a special right to
speak to this question, and is a justification for quot-
ing him once again: 'There is the constantly recurring
question whether we shall know and meet and recognise each other on the other side of death. One thing
is quite certain. Christian orthodoxy does not teach
the immortality of the soul; it teaches the resurrection of the body. We do not mean by that the resurrection of the body as it is. . . We would never wish
for the resurrection of a body with which a man was
smashed up in an accident or died with an incurable
disease. It so happens that Greek has no word for
personality, and the resurrection of the body means
the survival of the personality: It means that "In the
life beyond you will still be you, and I will still be
I."'

When death comes

With such a hopeful message in mind we can pass now
with confidence into what was called, in the Prologue
to this book, 'the quite unnecessarily darkened room
in which death and its attendant phenomena, like
props for an occasionally performed mystery play,
are usually stored'. What do we find there, then, once
a light is turned on? We find first of all some practical
consequences, usually affecting the next of kin.

Say, for example, that a man has died in hospital,
during the night. In the morning the hospital will ring
his next of kin, who may well be his wife. One need

for her, or for someone acting for her, will be in due course to return to the hospital to collect the medical certificate, an essential document without which a death cannot be registered. There may be some delay in the issuing of this. But it is always eventually forthcoming. This gives the cause of death. If there is any doubt about that, a post mortem may be necessary; but the hospital will need to have consent, indicated by the signing of a form. There is no mystery about a post mortem, nothing sinister about it, nothing to be afraid of.

The words mean 'after death'. The person who does it is a pathologist, who carries out a detailed examination of the body with the object of establishing medically why the person died. A post mortem is sometimes called an autopsy, which means 'seeing with one's own eyes'. It clearly has medical benefit in checking the accuracy or otherwise of the diagnosis of the dead person's final illness. It can be of much legal importance if the cause of death is in any way doubtful, or when it has been accompanied by unexplained circumstances. The process does not outwardly disfigure the body, and much care is usually given to the restoration of it to a normal appearance. There are sometimes objections on the grounds of improper interference with the body of a loved person. But in christian terms such objections cannot be sustained. It is true that Paul asks: 'Do you not know that your body is a temple of the Holy Spirit within you, which you have from God?' (1 Cor. 6.19). But the body is a temple when the spirit is within it. After death this is not so.

Before the body is removed from the ward to the hospital mortuary certain necessary procedures are carried out. This is because when a person dies the the body is subject to the process called rigor mortis, a stiffening caused by physiological changes. It begins about six hours after death, is complete in twelve, and lasts for twelve. In thirty-six hours it has gone. One practical consequence is that, shortly after death, the body needs to be 'laid out', which usually means straightened out and composed, in addition to being subject to certain elementary medical measures. Then a label is attached for identification purposes, and the body is wrapped in a shroud before being taken to the mortuary. Personal effects are gathered together and returned to the family eventually.

Some differences in procedure are necessary when a person dies at home. In this case the doctor who has been attending has to be told what has happened. He will then probably call. In any event he is the man who has to issue the medical certificate. If he has been treating the case some time and expecting the end, he may well have no particular problems about stating what, to the best of his belief, has been the cause of death. If he is in any doubt, or has not seen the patient for fourteen days, there may need to be a post mortem or possibly an inquest after the Coroner has been informed. Otherwise, the doctor will give the certificate to a member of the family, or leave it for collection at his surgery, or send it direct to the Registrar by post. His duty, unless those other matters arise, leading to an inquest, or unless there is a request for cremation, is now done and he can bow out.

Admittedly, all this, in its stark, matter of fact reality, can easily grate upon the sensitivities of someone recently torn by grief. The saving grace is that all can be wrapped around in prayer. That is the continuous contact which faith makes possible between those who are left and those who have gone. There are three kinds of prayer especially valuable at such a time as this.

The first is one which commends the soul of the departed to the loving care of God. To be informed by a phone call from a hospital that, for instance, one's husband, or wife or other close companion has died, is a bleak enough experience. But the moment can be transfigured by a prayer. The simplest and briefest form of words will suffice. Whether the prayer is spoken aloud or in the mind does not really matter, so long as it comes from the heart. Here is a lovely little prayer, easily remembered: 'Grant, to him, Lord, eternal rest, and let light perpetual shine upon him'. Or this, hallowed by much use: 'May the soul of the faithful departed, through the mercy of God, rest in peace'.

The second kind of prayer precious when death comes is that which gives thanks for all that has been lovely and good to be remembered in the life which is over. For example: 'Thank you, Lord, for . . . Thank you for all the good times we had together. Keep me confident that we shall meet again'.

And, thirdly, there is the prayer of acceptance of God's will in what has happened, without bitterness. Five words can say it all. 'Your will be done, Lord'.

This same, prayer-enwrapped attitude of mind will also make all the difference to the contact now necessary to be made with a person very important to all that is to be arranged. This is the funeral director. If this particular death had taken place at home instead of in hospital, he would have been able to arrange for the same 'laying out' at the house as was in fact done at the hospital. Incidentally, he would call this process 'the first offices', whereas to the hospital they would be the 'last offices'.

Whenever death comes he is one of the principal figures on the scene. Let us therefore turn some light on him. The kind of man he is, and the integrity and decency of the service he has to offer, is an important christian concern. Few may want his work; but it is fortunate for society that some do. His manner and tact can make all the difference to people in sorrow. He is a professional; he is in business; he is called upon not to share sorrow, which clearly with sincerity he cannot do, but to show respect for the sorrows of others. And he is absolutely essential. A funeral could scarcely take place without him, and few in fact ever do.

In essence, his is a disposal service. In the course

of carrying it out he is called upon to stage-manage funerals, as well as making all preliminary arrangements, subject to the wishes of those concerned, and for guiding through the complexities of all that needs to be done at such a time as this. He is not there to say what will happen; but rather to make it possible for it to happen when he receives his instructions. In practice, he often has to go beyond this brief, especially when dealing with people of no religious background who can find themselves totally lost in a strange land, with no terms of reference.

A funeral director interviewed for the purposes of this book was asked the same question as was put to various medical personnel, involved with the dying. 'What difference does religious belief make?' In this instance, obviously, the question related to those who had to be concerned with the consequences of a death. His reply was that it made a great deal. He said: 'You can tell in the first ten minutes of the first interview whether people know where they are in that respect'. He also commented that people unprepared in any way for death often reacted in the first instance with anger, as though so untoward an event should not have happened to them.

His premises were on the edge of the market area of an old town. There were large black cars being washed in the garage space adjoining. The window contained photographs of some of these vehicles, together with a vase of flowers. In nature and purpose this was the same kind of place visited by the journalist quoted earlier, who found the experience so extremely disturbing. But there was certainly nothing disturbing about this place, or the man. Both were matter of fact, helpful, and constructive. His wife, who was also qualified, worked with him. He spoke of the first interview which he or one of his staff would have with representatives of a bereaved family. Everything started with this. It could take place either at their house, or on his own premises. Most people contacted him by phone and they were always offered a personal call. Indeed, during the course of this interview, the phone rang four times and two people appeared in the office outside for an interview.

This would need to be detailed in order that he could be in full possession of all the facts, such as the name and age of the dead person, the place where the body was lying, the wishes of the family as regards time and place of the funeral, and methods of disposal of the body, by burial or cremation. He said that it would be likely, as a preliminary, that the relatives would prefer the body to be brought from the hospital, or, if the death had taken place at home, from the house to his own premises where it would be placed in what he called the 'Chapel of Rest'. It was a growing practice for this to happen. It had obvious advantages. All, or at any rate most, bodies nowadays were subject, he said, to what he called 'hygenic' or 'preservative' treatment. This was nothing to do with 'embalming' as commonly understood. It consisted principally of using a preservative fluid to arrest the processes of decay, with their attendant phenomena, and also restore the body in appearance as a comfort to those who had known and loved the person in life. He did emphasise, however, that there was no question of the extravagent cosmetic treatments sometimes practised as satirised in Evelyn Waugh's famous book *The Loved One*.

He said that people often wished to come and see the body in his Chapel of Rest before the coffin was closed. This raises the question, of whether, in christian terms, there' is a case for it. There are several reasons why the answer could be 'yes'. In the first place it is an act of affection: a little gesture towards what is now the outer shell of someone we knew once filled with life. Secondly, it is recognition not only of the reality of death; but also of the fact that we are not afraid to look upon it. In the past it was very much the custom to 'view' in this way. The development of the packaged, get-it-over-with-quick funeral so typical of today's world, is a recent development. But this is not necessary, and to look upon a body is right and proper.

But here again the experience can be greatly enriched by prayer. Here is an admirable one: 'Lord, to your gracious care we commit this body, asking that, as it is now sown a natural body it may be raised a spiritual body, through your power, who died and was buried and rose again for us, Jesus Christ our Lord'. Or, more simply: 'Thank you, Lord, for all that this body has meant to me, and help me to remember and believe that the soul has gone from it to you'.

The question of a choice between burial or cremation as a means of disposing of a body is a matter of basic christian importance. It is simple enough to make a decision on the grounds of expediency. But for the Christian expediency is not enough. The question involves a consideration of what we think about the human body, and what we believe about the spirit of which it is, in this world, the abiding place. It was out of confusion on those grounds that, after it was introduced in the nineteenth century, cremation was strongly opposed. It was seen as being totally destructive of the body which was to partake ultimately of a resurrection. How could it so partake if it were destroyed? There were other objections; but this was the main one. As Baring-Gould's hymn, a favourite with Victorians, put it:

'On the resurrection morning
Soul and body meet again.'

Such literal interpretation overlooks Paul's teaching that the resurrection body will be quite other than the physical. 'What is sown in the earth as a perishable thing, is raised imperishable. Sown in humiliation, it is raised in glory'. (1 Cor. 15.42).

The burning of a body in any event only speeds up a process which in the ground goes more slowly, but just as surely. The Burial Service in the Prayer Book has always made this clear in the lovely words, spoken as the body is lowered into the grave: 'Earth to earth, ashes to ashes, dust to dust'. What matters is the phrase which follows: 'In sure and certain hope of the resurrection to eternal life through our Lord Jesus Christ who shall change the body of our low estate that it may be like unto his glorious body'. Yet none of this seems to have prevented a bishop of Rochester in the eighteen-seventies from forbidding the building of a crematorium on consecrated ground. Less than a hundred years later the bodies of two Archbishops of Canterbury, Lang and Temple, were themselves cremated. And Roman Catholic objections were removed when, in 1963, the Pope declared the practice no longer prohibited.

What has brought about this change? A good development has been a better understanding, or at any rate a less literal interpretation, of the relationship between body and spirit and of a bodily resurrection. Much less desirable has been a tendency to want to get rid of the body as expediently as possible in order that, as part of the modern tendency of death-evasion, it may also be out of mind. The process of cremation is certainly expeditious. There need be no mystery about it. When the coffin descends from the chapel where the funeral service has been held, it is taken to the cremator, and it is placed in that small chamber unopened. Coffin and body are then consumed at very high temperatures, the process taking anything up to two hours. All that remains are ashes. Having been ground up to a fine powder, they can be scattered in the crematorium gardens, or returned to the relatives. What are they to do with them?

The question is not unimportant. Because cremation has made it possible to do things with human remains which would obviously not be feasible with a body, some strange practices have emerged. Golfers have had their ashes scattered on the fairway of their club. Some have been scattered on mountains where the deceased once walked or climbed. An American admiral is reported to have had his shot out of the torpedo tube of a submarine cruising at periscope depth under the Florida Straits! Whether such practices are dignified is for those personally concerned to judge. As far as the Church of England is concerned they are definitely discouraged by Canon Law. What they do show is a modern superstition that somehow the spirit of the departed is being gratified or made happy by them. A sensible principle to have in mind as regards disposal of this mortal clay is that anything which is tender and dignified is good; but that anything which encourages the idea that the departed is personally somehow 'there' is to be avoided.

But for the Christian, again, this does not go far enough. The human body, perishable as it may be, is a creation of God. It is a marvellous organism, a divine masterpiece through which human personality, its laughter its tears and its lovings, has expressed itself. Francis called his body 'Brother Ass', because it had so patiently born his burdens as it had carried him through the years. The human body, therefore, is worthy of profound respect, in death as in life. This is a very different thing from regarding it with super-stition. It is also a very different thing from the atti-tude which thinks it best to be unconcerned about what happens to the body once the last words have been said. It does matter.

The abrupt discontinuance of anything connected with the dead is one of the many factors which have made death seem not less awful but more so. it emphasises the sense of a blank end. A woman who, after the cremation of her husband in a large city crematorium, said to me she found the most shatter-ing experience was the sense of going away from it with nothing whatever to focus her grief upon, was voicing a very genuine and contemporary difficulty. Great burdens of secret grief can be placed upon people who are encouraged in the view that it simply does not matter what becomes of a loved one's body. It does — for them. People need some focus for their memories and affections. The old country custom of putting flowers on graves at Easter, thereby express-ing a continuing love in association with a place has much to recommend it. This can still be done, and the increasing practice of reserving an area in church-yards for the burial of ashes can do much to revive this old sense of loved people still having 'a local habitation and a name'. And such a practice also helps to meet the christian need to show 'respect', in the best sense, to the human body as a work of God, a temple of the Holy Spirit.

In christian terms, then, the choice between burial and cremation raises no matter of *principle,* provided that the body is treated with a decent reverence. The same consideration applies equally, of course, to burial. But in either case it is important, as already said, to avoid anything which suggests that the soul is somehow still to be identified with the place where the body or ashes ultimately rest. This feeling, admittedly, does linger. The very word 'cemetery' comes from a Greek word meaning 'a sleeping place, or dormitory'. But it is to be resisted because it obviously cannot be reconciled with a belief in a totally new beginning, in another order of being, once the gate of death has been passed and the soul has moved on. The abiding place of human remains, whether as ashes or body has significance, even so, because of what it can do for the living, not for the dead.

What does raise a matter of profound christian principle is the funeral service. It is of the highest importance that this should be meaningful, and it is sad when it is not. Therefore how can it be made significant? A good beginning is to think a little about what exactly is the purpose of such a service at all. When the Liturgical Commission, an expert group concerned with the modernisation and re-framing of Anglican Liturgies, came to consider this point they defined five principal purposes:

101

'To secure the reverent disposal of the corpse, to commend the deceased to the care of our Heavenly Father, to proclaim the glory of our risen life in Christ here and hereafter, to remind us of the aweful certainty of our own coming death and judgement, and to make plain the eternal unity of all christian people, living and departed, in the risen and ascended Christ'.

But how is this to be made to work in practice? There are several things which can be done to bring that about, and thereby to make the service reverent, memorable, and comforting. The first concerns the place. Whenever possible it should be held in church, rather than in the impersonal surroundings of a cemetery or crematorium chapel. The latter especially only too often gives an impression of being synthetic, like the taped muzak before and after. Practising Christians who can have the use of their own parish church (so can others, for that matter, if they wish), and the services of their own minister can avoid these depressing features. And to have a funeral service in a church where the dead person has worshipped is to make it possible for those who have shared that worship to feel very close in the bonds of the spirit and the communion of saints. So cemetery or crematorium are best used for the committal only, the service being held beforehand in church.

Secondly, there is the matter of the tempo, or pace of the service. It need not be prolonged; but it should not be hurried. It can be very disturbing and depressing to feel, as can happen at a big city crematorium, say, that there is another funeral outside waiting, and another after that. In church the pace can be easier, the pressure less, and time allowed for prayer and reflection.

Thirdly, there is the question of the content of the Service. What the Book of Common Prayer (1662) calls The Order for the Burial of the Dead, has served many generations well, and its words, as well as its beautiful cadences, are full of christian significance to those with the background to understand what they are saying. The new Series 3 Service, simplified and modernised, will no doubt with the passage of time find the same acceptance. It provides too for the funeral of a child. This new order also has a short service for use in the home before the service in Church. Here is a revival of what was once quite a general custom — a little gathering of close relatives of the dead before going on to the more public service. It can be helpful indeed to hear at such a time such a message as this of Paul's: 'For I am sure that neither death, nor life, nor angels, nor powers, nor things present, nor things to come, nor height, nor depth, nor anything else in creation, will be able to separate us from the love of God in Christ Jesus our Lord'. (Romans 8.31b:39) Such things can be remembered and treasured.

These services all provide for readings from the Scriptures, for Psalms, and for prayers. Such is their basic content. To this can be added music, which is always an enrichment, and can say things which words cannot. It helps, too, to give care to the choice of hymns, and to avoid anything which cannot be readily sung by all.

There are, however, two areas in which these services can fail to meet the needs of the occasion. Both failures arise from the manner of their use. The first comes, quite simply, from lack of preparation. The purposes of the funeral service as defined are fairly complex. The language in which these purposes are expressed, however modernised, needs thinking about if its various messages, of reverence, of hope, of unity in Christ of the living and departed, are to get across. So to go unprepared into such an occasion, unfamiliar with its order, as well as burdened by grief, and to expect its meaning to be clear is asking a lot. A simple remedy may well be to revive the old custom, once quite common, of reading through the service privately at home before taking part in it in Church. The awkwardnesses of the unfamiliar can thereby be rubbed away, the mind freed to receive with understanding the message proclaimed.

The second difficulty arising from the use, or rather mis-use, however innocently, of the Funeral Rite, is much more serious and far more difficult to remedy. This service was designed by Christians for Christians and yet is in fact used over and over again, as a matter of form, by non-Christians. How then can it possibly be expected to be meaningful for all and sundry? There was a raw moment in the celebrated

T.V. Documentary programme of some years ago called *Gale is Dead,* when the body of the pitiful, drug addicted girl who gave her name to the programme was brought to be cremated. After the service a woman who had tried to help her, and who had been present, heartbroken, complained bitterly that the officiating clergyman 'had not said anything at all'. The service had been meaningless. But what else could he have done but go by the book, apart from showing the sympathy which he did, and which was clearly all that was possible, to a party of mourners who had come out of the anonymity of the great city and who afterwards no doubt returned thereto? The book — the Burial Service — is very fine for those with the necessary background. But it is hard to think of any thing which could be expected to speak significantly to those with none. And yet the need for love and sympathy is agonisingly present always.

This difficulty may also arise in matters of conscience. There was, for instance, the widow of a man whose husband had not found it possible to accept any religious faith who found herself in difficulties when it came to his funeral service. These difficulties she expressed in a letter to a national magazine at the time. She felt it would be an affront to the views he had held — although she did not share them herself — to have the customary service. Yet to find an alternative proved hard indeed. But she was right, surely, to question the propriety of using a rite which she knew he would not have been able in principle to accept. There are solemn moments in life, and in death, where no one, by custom or convention, should be required to make statements, or hear things said, which they feel inappropriate. By the same token the christian service should not be put to uses and laid open to misunderstandings for which it was never designed. After all, it was made for people who can accept the statements of belief which it makes, and was framed at a time when most did.

But that no longer applies. So some find it unsatisfactory, not because it is meaningless; but because it has never come their way to give a thought to its meaning. In today's culture, where christian language and statements are not part of general experience, this can be the case with many. Time honoured and beautiful phrases such as 'Blessed are those who mourn, for they shall be comforted', or 'The Lord is my shepherd, therefore can I lack nothing', need some background of familiarity before they can come across with effect. Otherwise they are just noises or even, in some cases irritants, which is unfair to all concerned. This is surely another matter for christian concern.

The situation could be remedied, or at any rate helped, by having a secular funeral service available as an alternative. Sincere Christians could welcome this as a means whereby what is sacred to them would be less often misused by those to whom it is virtually without significance. The non-Christian could welcome it as a way out of a situation where they feel their sincerity compromised. And a vast majority who give no thought to the matter until a death in the family has caught them unprepared, but whose sorrows are just as important as anybody else's, and whose need for comfort just as great, could find that at least they have a choice about the kind of service they wish, sacred or secular. It is an interesting point that marriage, in this respect, has been provided for. There is the registry office service for those who do not wish for a Church wedding. Could there not be an equivalent for those who prefer not to have a 'Church Funeral'?

In practice, this does not seem to be easy to come by. Enquiries made at a large London crematorium brought the reply that anyone could opt for what was rather oddly called 'a non-Service service'. But the question was obviously regarded as strange. Every effort would be made, they said, to give people what they wanted in this respect. But they would need to be told. Otherwise, they would go 'by the book'. And this, except in the case of other religions, or of other christian communions, was that provided in those small black books in the chapel of any cemetery or crematorium — the Prayer Book Service for the Burial of the Dead, or, in some cases, its modernised form.

Yet there is in fact a secular service available, even though few know of it. The British Humanist Association (13 Prince of Wales Terrace, London W.8.) provides one, if asked. A comparison between this and the Christian rite is deeply interesting. This Humanist

Service begins with some impressive words, of which this is an example: 'Against all else it is possible to provide security; but against death all of us mortals alike dwell in an unfortified city'. Those present are then invited to show 'feeling for our lost friend. Not by lamentation but by meditation'. After that comes a period of silence, and then a spoken tribute to the dead person. Next there are some words to be said after the commital of the body: 'Here in this last rite, immune now to the changes and chances of our mortal lot, we remember his (or her) life; in gratitude we recall the human image he (or she) has given us. And now let us return to our own part in the world, that those who still live in it may have life more abundantly'.

This at least, is an honest attempt to provide an alternative to the christian rite, though whether it would be more effective in such a case as the funeral of Gale in *Gale is Dead,* or in any other such emotionally highly charged situation is open to question. Perhaps only personal ministration, based on close knowledge of those involved, could do anything in such a case.

But the christian rite says more, simply because there is more to say, since it is concerned with God, and with the christian hope of the life of the world to come. Clearly, it can be vastly comforting to hear, in the presence of the body of someone close and dear, such words as: 'We know that if the earthly frame that houses us today should be demolished, we possess a building which God has provided — a house not made by human hands, eternal and in Heaven'. (2 Cor. 5.1). But it has to be believed first. The essential step from being momentarily comforted to finding lasting truth in the face of death is the step of faith. Not everyone finds that possible or understandable. The Christian should have an equal concern for their sorrows, as well as for the right use of those sacred truths which can turn his own into joy.

So, when death comes, to make something memorable of the funeral service is of the highest importance. Some may wish to precede it by a celebration of Holy Communion, and both the Prayer Book Rite, and the Series 3 alternative make provision for this. A communion in church on the morning of the funeral can be intensely rewarding. The veil between the dead and the living becomes thin indeed in the presence of the Holy mysteries. There is a marvellous prayer of John Donne's which can be apposite at such a time, as we seek to share with the departed an experience which is already theirs.

'Bring us, O Lord God, at our last awakening into the house and gate of Heaven, to enter into that gate and dwell in that house, where there shall be no darkness nor dazzling: but one equal light: no noise nor silence, but one equal music: no fears nor hopes, but one equal possession; no ends nor beginnings, but one equal eternity; in the habitation of thy glory and dominion, world without end.'

On the lychgate of Sandringham Parish Church in Norfolk, through which the bodies of kings have passed before being taken thence to the pomps of a State funeral, there is a quiet reminder that death, timely or untimely, is for all. There are four Latin words: *Hodie mihi; cras tibi.* They mean: 'Today, to me: tomorrow to you'. Meanwhile, between that day and that tomorrow there is, for those who are left, a period which can be negative or creative; an end or a beginning. This is the time of bereavement, and it is part of looking at death to look at that also, because the one is a consequence of the other.

BEREAVEMENT

I walked a mile with Pleasure
She chattered all the way,
But left me none the wiser
For all she had to say

I walked a mile with Sorrow
And ne'er a word said she,
But oh, the things I learned from her
When Sorrow walked with me!

Facing the facts

The first words of this book were spoken by a woman recently bereaved: 'It's been such a shock'. She went on to add, although it was not mentioned at that point: 'Things can never be the same again'. She was quite right, even though in fact she was uttering them out of the depths, not only of grief, but also out of astonishment that a bereavement could seem to lay waste all that life had been. Yet to think of the experience in this shattered way is to make a desolation out of something which can be both creative and enobling, if faced with understanding.

Certainly, things would never be the same again for this woman. Nothing could recreate the life she had known when her husband was alive. The real question is what she would make out of the new situation now that he was dead. That is a basic question which faces all as they enter their own particular valley of the shadow at the death of someone dear and close. It cannot be answered until some of the facts about that valley are faced.

The rewards of such a facing of facts are rich indeed; for they can help not only with our own bereavements, when they come; but also with those of other people. The need in this area is great. Sorrow arising from bereavement, one of the most universal of emotional states, is at the same time one of the least understood. Geoffrey Gorer sums it up: 'Mourning is treated as if it were a weakness, a self indulgence, a reprehensible bad habit instead of a psychological necessity.' For the Christian, at least, that can never be enough. If Christ himself wept at the grave of his friend, (John 11.35) and said 'Blessed are those who mourn, for they shall be comforted' (Matthew 5.4), no follower of his should shrink from venturing among such shadows with such words of comfort as he can offer.

That does not mean that the shadows will necessarily go away. There are whole areas of the death experience where, as we have tried to show, the light of knowledge can indeed make them less dark. But bereavement is the exception. It has to be faced: its sorrows need to be recognised: its emotions given free rein. Healing lies in expression, not in repression. Colin Murray Parkes in *Bereavement, Studies of Grief in Adult Life* puts it well when he says: 'The pain of grief is just as much a part of life as the joy of love; it is perhaps, the price we pay for love, the cost of commitment. To ignore this fact, or to pretend that it is not so, is to put on emotional blinkers which leave us unprepared for the losses that will inevitably occur in our lives and unprepared to help others to cope with the losses in theirs'.

To lay those wise words alongside a specifically christian statement of the same truth is to see at once how closely the two correspond. Here, then, is Father Raymond Raynes, writing twenty years ago in *Darkness No Darkness:* 'There will be sorrow in any Christian life — godly sorrow, not depression and despair and low spirits: but godly sorrow, the very sorrow of Jesus, who was sad in the presence of death and of the sufferings of mankind; godly sorrow, in which as it were, we put our tiny drops of sorrow into that cup which our Lord drained to the dregs. But there is joy — joy in the knowledge of redemption . . . joy in the Communion of Saints, our brothers and sisters in Christ: the joy that comes from obedience . . . There is, too, the joy of anticipation, the looking into Heaven, hearing our Lord's invitation, "Come!" our Lord said: "I go to prepare a place for you. If it were not so I would have told you", "that where I am you may be also". This is the ultimate joy which eases the sorrows we must bear'.

This necessity of sorrow is, then, one of the major facts to be faced about bereavement. A further truth is that it is, in its own way, an illness. The terminology in which it is so often spoken of reveals this fact. Thus we speak of bereavement as a 'blow', of sorrow as a 'wound', which time may or may not 'heal'. Bereaved people are also by custom treated as though they were ill: expected to take time off work; spoken of and to in hushed tones, as though in a sick-room; relieved as far as possible of tasks and decisions. Then eventually the 'illness' is regarded as over, and the convalescent encouraged to return to normal life, much as someone who has, say, broken a leg, is urged to try and walk again on it. Indeed, so close is bereavement to being an illness that it can produce physical symptoms, of which sleeplessness, or loss of weight, or even gain of weight, or anxiety-states requiring drug therapy, including the use of anti-depressants, are but a few. A high proportion of a group of widows studied in this connection were discovered to have consulted their doctor within a few weeks of bereavement.

But what of the emotional consequences? Murray Parkes distinguishes two, both of the greatest concern to any who would seek to understand and help the bereaved. They are stigma and deprivation. What is the first of these? Several women interviewed for the purposes of this book, when asked what their first reactions had been to the loss of their husbands, gave, perhaps unconsciously, a definition of stigma. All said they felt that they had experienced a loss of status. They were diminished in the world. And though people were kind, they were also pitying which, for the person on the receiving end, was itself belittling. Or at least, they had found it so. One of those widows, indeed, had found this so trying that she had been moved to pull up all her roots of old associations and to make a new life for herself abroad. She was in fact discovered living on a Mediterranean island.

It helps to understand something of the origins of this strange phenomenon because it can then be explained and looked at charitably. Basically, then, stigma arises from fear — the fear of death. That is why, in some primitive societies, widows have been treated as taboo, as far as possible and for a time not to be approached; but isolated in a place by themselves. This is how one such society, as described by a writer quoted by Murray Parkes, treated their widows: 'She may only go out at an hour when she is unlikely to meet anyone, for whoever sees her is thought to die a sudden death. To prevent this she knocks with a wooden peg on the trees as she goes along, warning people of her presence. It is believed that the very trees on which she knocks will soon die'.

Very deep, therefore, lie the roots from which comes stigma. There have been societies where it has even been considered proper that a widow should die with her husband, as witness the ritual suicide customs once common in wide areas of Asia and Africa. The British in India long ago had great difficulty for instance in suppressing the practice of Suttee, whereby a widow was supposed to immolate herself on her husband's funeral pyre.

Any widow who senses now the gradual withdrawal of her former friends, and a general avoidance of her company is experiencing something of this strange and ancient aversion. Sometimes it is even encouraged by the woman herself, who withdraws from company, as if shrinking into a shell. Another of those interviewed on this matter said that she had for a long time after her husband's death felt an over-mastering desire to be alone. The same person also, at about the same time, set out by herself to drive to Italy, something she would never have undertaken when her husband was living. It was as if she needed to prove to herself that she had experienced another common consequence of bereavement — a role change. She was a different personality, and was wise enough to recognise the fact. In such ways can a resolute character face up to stigma. But it is not easy. The greatest help which can be given by relatives and friends is love based on understanding of what the bereaved person is going through in these respects. Some of the ways in which that love can be expressed we shall see later.

Meanwhile, what of deprivation? This means loss — the loss of someone who has been a provider, a sustainer, a companion. Bereavement bears particularly hard at this point. The consequence of deprivation is loneliness, just as the consequence of loss is grief. This loneliness which, like stigma, has deep and ancient roots in human behaviour, is hard to bear. It is also likely to continue until the gaps in life left by it can be filled by other interests. This development is much to be encouraged, and offers a rewarding field for constructive help from others. It is of interest in this context that the same woman who had felt the need to embark on a solitary journey on the Continent soon after her husband's death, said several years later that she felt, regretfully, that he was now further away than he had been. The reason was probably that she had been successful in filling with other interests the gaps of loneliness which hitherto had been occupied solely by his memory.

But this is not easy. Not everyone can manage it. Widowers may find it even more difficult than widows, because they are usually in physical terms less able to look after themselves. And bereaved parents may find it most difficult of all, because the loss of a child presents special problems of grief, with accompanying emotions of guilt, remorse and anger against God and man. To express these griefs is vital, to accept these losses essential, because acceptance is always the way out of bitterness and back to the love of God. The Senior Nursing Officer of a famous hospital for children, speaking at a conference, contrasted the reactions of two couples each of whom had lost a child from leukemia. The first accepted the fact and were healed. The second failed to do so and were destroyed. In any event, to discover new opportunities of service for God's sake is often to create a strange new heaven out of what had been a hell.

There are two prayers in Michael Holling's and Etta Gullick's collection *The Shade of His Hand* which wonderfully express something of this desolation. One is on the death of a husband:

'How awfully alone! He's dead; and I loved him: but I never knew how much I loved him till he was dead. Oh! what a fool I've been. Oh God, let us meet again in you'.

The second is on the death of a son:

'I do miss my son so much, Lord. I loved cooking for him, mending his clothes and looking after him. I can't understand why you let him get killed so suddenly. He was hardly out of his teens. I'm lost without him and don't sense his presence near me at all, and I can't even visualise his being alive with you. There is an emptiness in my life. Show me how to live now, for it is very hard. I often think of your mother and how she must have felt after you had died on the Cross. . .

I wonder if you could ease my ache a little if you sent me someone else to look after. . .'

How that kind of prayer was anwered in one particular case was told, privately afterwards, by a broadcaster in a series of talks in the B.B.C's Thought for the Day spot on Radio 4. His theme had been the

118

importance of making something of one's life, something creative and good, however unfavourable the circumstances. One of his listeners, quite unknown to him, was a recently bereaved widow who had totally given up, overwhelmed by loneliness and desolation. The night before she had drunk herself to sleep, leaving the radio on. The first words which penetrated her stupor the next morning came from that radio. They spoke immediately to her condition. They penetrated the heart. So she got up, and went out into the grey day, as she described it later in her letter to the speaker, to find to what new use she could devote her days. She discovered the answer in visiting and caring for solitary old people, with whom, she found, the district abounded.

Such a happening may well not be exceptional, except for the curious circumstances of its inception. Many bereaved people do manage bravely to start again. But it is rarely easy to do so single handed. Help based on understanding sympathy is of great importance. It is therefore very much a Christian concern to consider some of the ways in which the bereaved can be helped.

Helping the bereaved

Just as it was found useful to think about what a concerned friend may expect to find, as regards physical and emotional states, in the dying, so it is of value to make a similar enquiry of the bereaved as a first step to helping them through what, as we have seen, is a very intense and testing experience. Obviously, because people and circumstances vary so much, there cannot be any set pattern to it. A sudden death may produce a shock in the bereaved severe enough to act as a kind of anaesthetic, so that the bereaved person may appear for a time so numbed as to be unable to express any emotion at all commensurate with the situation. Or it may be that they feel it actually wrong to show emotion, preferring rather to bottle it up. It is an odd fact about the way that we live now that we seem to find it so difficult to cope with sorrow. Thus a crying child in public is a matter for concern. But a crying adult anywhere is a fearful embarrassment, a solecism, almost an indecency. None of this makes it any easier to help the bereaved.

That mention of the crying child raises a matter of immense importance. It can never be forgotten that children are bereaved, that children have a work of mourning to do. The tendency to try to disguise from them what has happened can be both cruel and damaging. So can the temptation to fall back upon such obviously cosmetic statements as that 'Daddy has gone to Jesus'. Or that, maybe, a little sister has been 'taken to Heaven because God wanted her'. Gorer puts it: 'It is difficult to avoid the conclusion that a sizeable minority of British parents are using God and Jesus in communication with their children in exactly the same way as they use Santa Claus'. The fact is that hiding death from children can do great harm.

They know that it has happened. They must be helped, and it is often not so difficult as it is with adults. If a child is talked to lovingly, openly, and in terms which make religious sense, which should be possible for Christians, he will cope as far as his emotions permit.

There may be a period of fear, then of anger against the parent trying to explain matters, and then sometimes what appears to be a complete switch off back to normal interests. Perhaps teenagers need more special help, because obviously they are more developed. A young man with considerable experience of Christian counselling, on reading these words, added: 'I know one person who dates the loss of a real Christian faith from the death of her older brother, whom she secretly adored. She told me that everyone was so busy helping her parents that no-one, literally no-one, spoke to her about it. She went into the dark alone, and for good. I think it is best not to send children to school on the day of a funeral in the family. I've known it happen, with the best of intentions, and in a devout family. But when the child found out, she was heartbroken. She should have been told and at least allowed to have a different day — perhaps with some one else, but not too far from her fellow mourners. I myself would rather even let children go to the funeral. I've seen it done, wonderfully; but obviously it needs playing by ear'. It can be summed up by saying that perhaps the two greatest dangers, even maybe the two greatest sins, in the treatment of children and young people involved in a bereavement are falsity and secrecy.

To return to adults, when there has been a period of acute anxiety and suffering accompanying a last illness there may well come a sense of relief to the survivor which for a time can override sorrow. There can also be a determination not to face the fact of death so resolute as to lead to the self deception that it has not happened. A classic instance was the re-action of Queen Victoria to the loss of her husband. The Prince Consort's rooms, by her order, were left exactly as they had been during his life. Even his shaving things were set out, ready for use.

All these are abnormalities, however touching and sad. The fact is that mourning is a necessity if grief is to be overcome. Tears are good, as a blessed relief. Any embarrassment at the sight of them, or any dis-couragement of them, is much to be avoided, just as is revulsion at physical symptoms of illness. The christian duty is clear. Paul set it down in Romans 12.15; 'Rejoice with those who rejoice, weep with those who weep'. The wisdom of this godly advice was emphasised by such remarks as that of the American Doctor Erich Lindemann who, after a fire disaster in Boston, Massachusetts in 1943 set up a 'Grief Clinic' in his Hospital at which numbers of the bereaved attended. Speaking of the healing value of emotion he said that 'one of the big obstacles to this work seems to be the fact that many patients try to avoid the intense distress connected with the grief experience and the expression of emotion necessary to it. It follows that the apparent absence of such emotion should never be taken as an indication that grief is not present. It can often mean the exact opposite, which is an important truth to be remembered at first encounter with a bereaved friend or relative.

Other reactions are to be expected, and it is well to have these also in mind. People who have suffered a bereavement seem at times to imagine that they are somehow to blame for the death which has taken place. If only they had done this, or not done or said that, or if only someone else had acted differently. The strange outburst of Mary after the death of Lazarus seems to echo this feeling: 'Oh Sir, if you had only been here my brother would not have died'. (John 11.32). Just so may some widow bitterly regret a possibly unkind remark to a husband who shortly afterwards died, and blame herself for it. Such feelings may be emotional; but they are certainly real, and add to a sense of guilt hard to cure.

Anger, too, is to be expected — anger against God sometimes, and therefore prone to be directed upon those supposedly representing him. The parents of a dead child mentioned in an earlier chapter, who turned with such hostility upon the parish priest when he called, were a case in point. Often this anger is a blind hitting out at anybody and anything, from the doctor supposed to have been at fault to the would-be comforter held to have said something false. Such anger needs to be understood, and endured.

Even Job turned upon his friends: 'I have heard many such things: miserable comforters are you all. Shall windy words have an end. . .?' (Job 16.2).

This kind of reaction was echoed in a remarkable statement by a Lincolnshire clergyman as reported in *The Guardian* Newspaper of 19.1.78: 'It is better for the bereaved to rant, rave and scream, even to go to church for the sole purpose of telling God how much they hate him, rather than bury anger and distress deep within themselves', he is reported to have said. 'Reserve and the stiff upper lip are not always the wisest things for mourners . . . they can turn inwards and develop long lasting depressions or great anxieties'. Those who have studied the psychology of bereavement would certainly seem to agree with these general conclusions.

There is also to be found in bereaved people the creation of an idealised image of the dead. They could do no wrong; they had qualities beyond compare; kind, loving, noble. This build-up of the character of a person who may well in life have been ordinary enough — though none the less dear — can amount almost to the creation of an idol enthroned in memory. Once again Queen Victoria provides an instance. Albert, the perfect, became almost a deified figure, to the worship of which she devoted years of her life, remaining meanwhile withdrawn from the world. There are Victorias and Alberts now, in sad abundance.

Depressions, loneliness, feelings of insecurity are

likewise to be encountered in this shadowed country. Everyone who has loved and lost must expect to spend some time there. But not too long. There must, if life is to renewed, come the time of an emergence again. How long bereavement lasts will obviously vary greatly from person to person. Professional guesses, such as that of Freud, who held that six months was an acceptable duration, or Lindemann, who favoured six weeks, have an unreal air about them. Nobody can know, because everyone is different.

Some primitive societies have signified the fact that a period of mourning must have an end by designating one year after the death as a time for a 'second burial'. In one such East African community an image of the dead person is placed within the tomb, facing in the opposite direction from that in which the body is lying. The significance intended is that the dead person, who for a year has been openly mourned, has now gone to join his ancestors. Those who are left are free to begin their lives again, and the emphasis changes from sorrow to rejoicing. Maybe we could use such a helpful approach in our own so called civilised society, where comparatively little thought seems to be given to such matters.

Meanwhile, bereaved people sometimes seem to know in their hearts when a true 'break away' moment has come, and they feel released from the prison of their grief. In one case known to this writer it was, for a youngish woman who had lost her husband, the first time she went out with another man.

In another — the woman already mentioned who ended up living abroad — it was when the decision had been taken to go.

There is nothing heartless about such acts. Nobody can live in emotional solitary confinement for ever, even when the cell is self made and adorned with an image of the deceased. Life must go on, and the choice is always between going with it or being left behind. But, blessedly, for the Christian with a strong sense of the timeless bond which unites living and dead, this never need or should involve a leaving behind of memories or any dwindling of the hope of meeting again. The continuing link between the two worlds of the living and the dead is prayer. It can be rewarding indeed to give imaginative thought to its best use. A man who had lost a young wife drew much comfort from setting aside each anniversary of their wedding and her birthday for special spiritual commemoration, beginning with a Communion at which he both knew and felt he was meeting with her. Age cannot wither nor custom stale such lovely acts. It does no violence to Paul's phrase: 'I thank my God in all my remembrance of you' (Philippians 1.3), to remember that it can be used for the dead as well as for the living.

The continuing question, however, facing those who seek to help the bereaved is how best they may do so. Lily Pincus, in her wise book *Death and the Family*, makes the valuable point that somebody's loss is, or should be everyone's concern. 'It affects the community in which the loss occurred, and the bereaved needs the understanding and support of the community. In the past, community support found expression in rituals. These *rites de passage* gave sanction to mourning, helping the bereaved to make adjustments to the world in which she had to live without the lost person'.

Looked at in this light, the story of the widow who, having spent the night in a drunken stupor, was accidently recalled to life by a speaker on the radio, is a reflection far more on the community in which she lived than upon the woman herself. She should not have been left alone like that. God alone knows how awful bereavement must sometimes be in those parts, such as great housing estates or inner cities or self exclusive suburbs, where a sense of community simply does not exist. Too often there is only the doctor's surgery left, with some pills as a substitute for the love and support which friends could give. And alcohol, a potent drug indeed, can be far more dangerous because more easily available and less controlled.

It would be wrong, however, not to acknowledge that thought has in recent years been given to the special problems of the bereaved. Murray Parkes notes how, in Boston, Massachusetts, there exists a widows' aid programme started by a research Social Worker. The basic feature of this is that mature workers routinely call upon newly bereaved women living in their area. Their own fundamental qualification, although they are carefully selected, is that they are themselves bereaved and have adjusted to it. In Britain there is the CRUSE Organisation (named after the widow in 1 Kings 17 who had 'a little oil in a cruse', and whose son the Prophet Elijah subsequently revived from death). Its method is to bring together widows in mutual support, in CRUSE Clubs wherever they exist. It also endeavours to call upon the services of Clergy, Doctors and Social Workers prepared to advise bereaved women. (The emphasis upon women is statistically inevitable. Widows numerically far exceed widowers, just as the life expectancy of women exceeds that of men). For parents, male and female, who have lose children, The Society of Compassionate Friends aims to offer comfort and support, by putting like in touch with like, those bereaved of children, with others in the same situation.

But in practice it is often, with most people, in the two or three weeks after the funeral that grief strikes hardest. The 'excitement' is over; the need to show public composure is no longer there; those who came together for the occasion and maybe stayed on a while, have gone. Then comes the time for the noticeable silences in a house which once held another voice: then comes the time for the sitting alone in front of the television. That is the time, beyond any other for the helpful friend to be around.

To do what? Firstly, to be there. Secondly, to be imaginative of the needs of the bereaved to pour out

at will emotions which have been dammed up hitherto: of guilt, of grief, of helplessness. Thirdly, to be a
patient listener to it all, knowing that by doing so far
more healing work can be done than by any other
means. Fourthly, to be one who recognises that the
bereaved person has a work of mourning to do, and
needs to be helped to express it, not to suppress it. As
Autton observes 'instead of helping the bereaved to
get over their sorrow, it sometimes is wiser to help
them get into it, provided of course that we go down
with them into the valley of the shadow'.

Above all, as with visiting the sick — and helping
the bereaved is in a sense another form of the same
kind of ministry — it is vital to tread delicately in the
area of any overt attempts at spiritual consolation. A
mother can be stricken rather than comforted by
being told that her child is 'in heaven', if only because
the thought, to a nature made hyper-sensitive by
grief, makes him seem further away, not nearer. This
is not a time for religious, or, for that matter, any
other clichés. To urge a bereaved person to 'bear up'
is not helpful, either. Nor is any attempt to persuade
them to look upon what has happened as 'a happy
release'. It is not a happy release — for them. And
though it may seem natural to urge cheerfulness upon
the sorrowful, it can in fact be very much a wrong
approach. The bereaved need their sorrow, and to
mask it can only too easily come to seem a betrayal
of the dead. Similarly, any attempt to diminish the
experience they are going through by being philo-

sophic about it — 'it happens to everyone, you know', can be hurtful. A bereavement for the person concerned is a unique event, and it is no more a comfort for them to be reminded that it is a universal experience than it is for someone in severe pain to be told that many others suffer it, too.

But the way of the comforter is not all difficulty. There is much quiet satisfaction from realising how greatly simple yet imaginative acts of practical sympathy can help. A telephone call at a lonely hour can be a wonderful thing. Lily Pincus gives another instance: 'Saturday afternoons, which may have been a married couple's regular time for a joint outing, may be another vulnerable time. A friend of mine who had adjusted exceptionally well to her widowed life told me that, even years after her husband's death, she avoided being alone at home on a Saturday afternoon in order not to watch compulsively and with envy her married neighbours going out together'. How great could be the service of someone who, having realised this, would help by filling that Saturday afternoon gap!

Maybe it can all be summed up by saying that the secret of the comforter is love, which 'bears all things, believes all things, hopes all things, endures all things'. The reward may equally be to become unnecessary when, in God's good time, the bereaved may have emerged from the valley of the shadow in such a sound emotional state as to be able to face up to the next task which awaits them — that of making out of their situation a creative bereavement.

Creative bereavement

It is told of John Bright, the political reformer that, one day shortly after the death of his young wife, when her body was yet in the house, his friend Richard Cobden called to offer condolences. Bright, shattered by grief, received them dumbly. Then, after a pause, Cobden said: 'There are thousands of houses in England at this moment where wives, mothers and children are dying of hunger — hunger made by the Laws. When the first paroxysm of your grief is past, come with me, and we will never rest until those Laws are repealed'.

And that indeed was what happened. Out of a grief that could have been destructive Bright made a new life which was constructive in the highest degree. In other words, he began again. The story has a similarity to that of a woman who was moved by a radio talk to venture out into a new life after bereavement. It can be done. When it is done, then bereavement can truly be called creative. But it is not easy, and is a tough test of character. An exaggerated fear of loyalty to the departed can actually get in the way: the feeling that 'so and so would not have wished me to do this'. Yet, where true love has been present, it is surely fair to assume that the very opposite could be the case, and the desire of the dead for the living would be that they should succeed in having life, and having it more abundantly. One widow, whose husband had been a very able doctor, said that, in creating her own new life, she had been much motivated by the thought that he would feel let down by any weakness and failure on her part. 'Many people misjudge the permanent effect of sorrow and their capacity to live in the past', wrote Ivy Compton-Burnett in *Mother and Son*. It is a thoroughly sensible remark. Sorrow cannot be indefinitely prolonged, and the past is no place to linger when the future is possible. As Joshua Liebman memorably put it in his *Peace of Mind:* 'The melody that the loved one played upon the piano of your life will never be quite the same again; but we must not close the keyboard and allow the instrument to gather dust. We must seek out other artists of the spirit, new friends who will gradually help us to find the road to life again, who will walk that road with us'.

But for the Christian there need be no fear that in thus venturing into new paths the departed will be, as it were, left behind until with time they are out of sight and mind. The practice of the faith, with its constant reminder of the thinness of that veil which separates the living from the dead, with the strong promises of the Scriptures and the hope of the resurrection, is proof against that, if it is accepted with conviction and with a resolution to continue in it.

But it is well to give specific form to the expression of this in relation to the dead. Not for nothing was it the custom of the early Christians to remember them particularly at the altar. The man mentioned earlier in this narrative who in that way commemorated at Communion the anniversary of his dead wife's birthday and of their wedding was on the right lines. Such acts do more than give form and substance to a generalised hope. They bring the living and the dead closer than they are every likely to be anywhere else in this world. A poem of John Betjemen's *House of Rest* tenderly expresses it. An elderly widow, 'relict' as in the past they were fond of saying, of a long dead clergyman, is at Communion remembering him and the family they had together brought up:

> 'Now when the bells for Eucharist
> Sound in the market square,
> With sunshine struggling through the mist
> And Sunday in the air,
> The veil between her and her dead
> Dissolves and shows them clear.
> The Consecration Prayer is said
> And all of them are near. . .'

It remains true, however, that bereavement is a tremendous and testing experience. Dean Inge in his *Personal Religion and a Life of Devotion*, a book which owed much to the death of his beloved young daughter, wrote 'bereavement is the deepest initiation into the mysteries of human life, an initiation more searching and profound than even happy love. Love remembered and consecrated by grief belongs, more clearly than the happy intercourse of friends, to the eternal world: it has proved itself stronger than death.

Bereavement is the sharpest challenge to our trust in God: if faith can overcome this, there is no mountain which it cannot remove'. With faith and hope, of course, must always go courage. That is a necessity. And anyone contemplating this task of making a new life, after a death has seemed to destroy an old one, may well have in mind, as they think of the difficulties, the words of Moses to his people trembling on the brink of crossing the Jordan: 'Be strong and of good courage, do not fear or be in dread of them. For it is the Lord your God who goes with you: he will not fail you or forsake you.' (Deuteronomy 31.6).

LIFE AFTER DEATH

Dear, beauteous Death! the jewel of the Just,
Shining nowhere but in the dark:
What mysteries do lie beyond thy dust,
Could man outlook that mark!

Henry Vaughan

It is time now to turn back, thoughtfully and tenderly, to those collections of family photographs we were dwelling upon in the first chapter of this book. 'There they are, reaching from today, to yesterday, to the day before yesterday. . . We can still in memory faintly hear their voices, and in the mind's eye hold blurring glimpses of their faces. . . The great question is "Where have they gone? Where shall we go?" ' As we saw then, the Christian hope of the life of the world to come is that alone which makes such questions worth facing, because it provides blessed assurance that death is not the end of us; but that in Christ we live, here and hereafter. Obviously, many questions remain. What will this hereafter be like? What is Heaven — and Hell, for that matter? How are we to think of these mighty concepts? And do the dead in any way communicate with us now?

Many, the well known, and the less known, in the past and in the present, have written round and about these timeless themes. It is useful to share a few of their thoughts with some of them, to pick a few flowers, as it were, from the great field where so many of them grow. W.R. Matthews, Dean of St. Pauls from 1934-67, in his book *Memories and Meanings*, has a striking passage upon how the truth of being 'risen with Christ', and therefore heirs to eternal life, can come on us quite unexpectedly in the course of everyday life:

'Have you noticed one rather strange thing about the appearance of the risen Christ to individuals? The two disciples on the road to Emmaus; the solitary figure in the mist by the lake; Mary Magdalen's impression of the gardener by the tomb. At first sight the Lord Jesus is not recognised, but soon there comes the "moment of truth" and the cry, "it is the Lord". It is as if the Master is disguised and is waiting for the disguise to be penetrated by the disciple. "The moment of truth . . ." Have you never had one when the eyes of your spirit were opened? I am talking, for example, to a person who seems quite commonplace and ordinary, and then something he says or does, some gesture or even some silence reveals to me that he is quite an extra-ordinary person; Christ is living in him, he is a living witness to the Risen Christ; and because the Christ in me responds we have our moment of truth and joy. I am strengthened and confirmed in my faith that Christ is risen and I am risen with him to eternal life'.

The French Abbé Henri de Tourville, wrote strongly of this eternal life as we have it now, and of how this consciousness of it should affect our attitudes to death. The passage comes in his *Letters of Direction* written during the last twenty years of his life. The book was eagerly welcomed and many people found light and comfort in it, and still do.

'Life limited by death? Nonsense! That is a great mistake. Death hardly counts; it is a mere appearance; we already have eternal life and that reflection should give us great tranquillity, as those who feel themselves to be eternal. Do not therefore be afraid of death. It is the flowering of life, the consummation of union with God. . . We must think of the dead as alive and joyful and we must rejoice in their happiness, remembering that we are in close and constant communion with them, our life only separated from theirs by the thinnest of veils. We must remember that this does not separate us either from God, our eternal joy, who more than makes up all that we lack — or from the companionship of those who are with God in infinite time and space. Let us be brave and keep the eyes of our souls wide open to all these realities: let us see clearly around us those things which others only care to see dimly.'

But what can we see? The question is as old as the hills, because men and women have always tried to look into the beyond. This is natural: but it is important to acknowledge our limitations. The pictures we try to make for ourselves of life in the beyond tend often to be idealised recreations of life as we know it here, with its sufferings and sorrows removed. Michael Perry, in *The Resurrection of Man,* has a helpful passage about this need for reticence concerning the details of the life to come:

'The first thing to acknowledge about the resurrected life is, in the words of Richard Baxter, that:

"My knowledge of that life is small,
The eye of faith is dim;
But 'tis enough that Christ knows all,
and I shall be with him."

'In other words, we must be reticent about the details. That we shall be happy and fulfilled has been expressed in many pictorial ways; golden streets, harps, wings, radiance — but these are only analogies and must not be taken for literal description. We cannot be specific. But that does not really matter. There is a familiar sermon illustration about a christian doctor at the bedside of a dying patient who knew he had only a short time to live, and who wanted to be told what exactly was ahead of him. The doctor refused to be drawn, saying that he could not be dogmatic about any of the details. He only knew that his patient was going to be with Christ.

'The patient complained that so vague an assurance was little comfort, so the doctor whistled softly. At the bedroom door there was a scratching noise, and he opened it. In came his dog, and nuzzled his face into the doctor's hand. The dog had never been in that room before. He knew nothing of what his surroundings were going to be like; but his master was there and was calling him, and that was sufficient reason for him to want to come through the door and into the unknown room, and for him to know that there he would be content.

'The Christian will want to exercise a reticence similar to that doctor when asked to give details of the future life. He will simply say that it is a matter of "things beyond our seeing, things beyond our hearing, things beyond our imagining, all prepared by God for those who love him" '. (1 Cor 2.9).

Such language as that of Paul is made more difficult for us, living in this present time, to comprehend and feel in the heart and soul, than probably at any time of human existence. This is because we live, move, and have our being, whether we like it or not, in a material age. In such an atmosphere, unless we are on our guard against it, the idea insidiously grows that only that which we can touch, or see, or otherwise physically apprehend is real. Such a way of thinking blocks off that which is spiritual; unheard, unseen; but none the less blazingly real. To accept unthinkingly a material view of life is to deny to ourselves vast areas of imaginative understanding of life and death which have been the precious possession of generations before us. Fortunately, there are some signs of a reaction against an excessively material view of the human experience. People are beginning to reach out and explore in long neglected areas. One of them is psychical research. Here, for instance, is a passage from a recent book in that area *Believe it or Not,* by Chancellor Garth Moore, President of the Churches' Fellowship for Psychical and Spiritual Studies.

'Psychical research does show that it is more probable that the Christian Doctrine of the life everlasting is true. At the lowest estimate, psychical research shows that survival of bodily death is more probable than extinction, and some of the evidence shows that such survival is much more probable. This, for those who doubt, is a great leap forward. If survival of bodily death can be established, or even rendered probable, the great step forward has been taken. The next step, from mere survival to survival to all eternity, is a much smaller step. If survival at all occurs, it is not unreasonable to envisage it as going on forever or as being but one further stage in a process which goes on forever'.

He then touches upon that very point we noticed earlier — that concepts of time and space, being products of our physical existence, can be real limitations when we try to look into the beyond.

'This is all the more so having regard to our ignorance concerning the time factor. For all we know, time, as we understand it here, does not exist outside the material universe. It is, as it were, the framework for the material and can be shed together with the material, If however it does exist outside the material universe, it may exist in a form very different from anything that we can envisage, and the words eternal and everlasting may have ceased to have meaning.'

But homely and understandable questions always exist when men and women think about life after death. Among the chief of them are: what is Heaven like? Do we meet again with those we have loved? Is there reality, in fact, in those wonderful lines of Newman's:

'And with the morn those angel faces smile,
Which I have loved long since, and lost awhile'

And what — because we cannot evade this question — are we to think of Hell, a formidable concept to which our forbears attached such great importance? Has so much taken place in human thinking, and in human knowledge of the universe of which we are a tiny part, since those days, which render this valueless now? Far from it, provided, that is, that we are prepared still to take the Scriptures as our guide. Thus we can safely say that Heaven is where God is, and Hell is where God is not. This is as true now as ever it was. It is even clearer to the understanding once we can dispense with the limitations of thinking in terms of time and space. The vision in Revelation is very relevant: 'And I saw the Holy City, New Jerusalem, coming down out of Heaven from God, prepared as a bride adorned for her husband; and I heard a loud voice from the throne saying, "Behold, the dwelling of God is with men. He will dwell with them, they shall be his people, and God himself will be with them; he will wipe away every tear from their eyes and death shall be no more, neither shall there be mourning nor crying nor pain anymore, for the former things have passed away" '. (Revelation 21.2-4)

As to Hell, there is one important respect in which modern knowledge, especially man's growing knowledge of himself through psychological insights, may well alter the idea of Hell as a state of being in which God punishes those who have sinned, to the concept of a state of being where the human personality, having entered the state where no pretence is possible, becomes aware for the first time of what his or her character really is. That could be a very terrible realisation. Too many of us are guilty of too many false pretences in this life to be immune from a fearful moment when those falsities are taken away. The medieval painters of 'doom' murals may have been too simplistic in showing Hell as a place to which a judgemental God consigns sinners. But it remains very much a possibility that Hell is a state in which self knowledge shows us for the first time what we are and throws us, maybe also for the first time, upon the hope of God's love and forgiveness. Seen in this light, Paul's words take on an even further profundity of meaning: 'For now we see in a mirror dimly, but then face to face. Now I know in part; then I shall understand fully, even as I have been fully understood.' (1 Cor 13.12.)

For those left on this side of the veil, the question

of communication with those who have passed beyond it ever looms large. It is bound to. Voices, appearances, strange hints that the departed from time to time are reaching out to us have been the experience of many people and continue to be so. But all those phenomena are best kept firmly within the framework of the Christian faith and hope which makes them possible. Never has this been more clearly stated than by William Temple who, having been consulted by a man who felt that he had experienced an appearance of his late wife, wrote in reply:

'I am deeply touched that you should consult me about this experience. I wish I felt more competent to help. I have always thought it a mistake to go into questions connected with spiritualism unless one could do it thoroughly; and for that I have had no time. But of course I have been interested and have reached some conclusions, which have, I regret to know, very inadequate bases. However, here they are:

1. I draw a sharp distinction between any experience which, like yours, is unsought, and anything resulting from resort to a medium or deliberate waiting for messages — e.g., by automatic writing; the latter so obviously makes opportunities for the subconscious mind to act.

2. So far as I have considered psychical phenomena, I know nothing that would persuade me to accept so

great a conclusion as survival of death if I did not believe it on other grounds; but as I do believe it on other grounds I am strongly inclined to interpret some of the phenomena as actual communication.

3. The evidence for appearances at the moment of death, or in a dream state at later times, of those who were very closely bound by love to the person concerned is stronger than for any other such communication.

'With that background of thought I am led by the description of your own experience to believe that it is a perfectly real communion between you and your wife, in which she took the first step by "coming" to you. It cannot be more than a "probable" judgement; but the probability seems to me to lie on that side rather than on the side of hallucination. I think therefore that you should think it both possible and even probable that the experience was due to an external cause, and that God did thus permit your wife to make known to you her love and (so far as that might be called for) her forgiveness.

'But all this rests on (a) faith in God and his care for us, (b) consequent faith in our survival of death and continued fellowship. And this order of priority is very important both for the logic of the belief reached and for the spiritual outlook of anyone who holds it. I was glad to see your phrase about God's permission to your wife to help you, because that shows that the right order of priority is in your mind.'

It was at the funeral of that very same William Temple, in Canterbury Cathedral in the October of 1944 that, strangely enough, the words of the Anthem sung, with unforgettable power and effect, were a poem in which the seventeenth century visionary Henry Vaughan drew a poet's picture of Heaven:

> My soul, there is a country
> Far beyond the stars,
> Where stands a winged sentry
> All skilful in the wars:
> There, above noise and danger,
> Sweet peace sits crowned with smiles,
> And One born in a manger
> Commands the beauteous files.
> He is thy gracious Friend,
> And — oh my soul awake! —
> Did in pure love descend
> To die here for thy sake.
> If thou canst get but thither,
> There grows the flower of peace,
> The rose that cannot wither,
> Thy fortress, and thy ease.
> Leave then thy foolish ranges;
> For none can thee secure
> But One who never changes —
> Thy God, thy life, thy cure.

Because of what we know of ourselves, never mind what we think we know of other people, which of us can ever suppose that we would be worthy to enter such a Heaven and to be with God? The very thought is overpowering. So is the question of those who have never heard of God, and therefore never even been in a position to reject him. Certainly, it is not for us to judge. But equally certainly it is for us never to forget that at the very heart and centre of the Christian Gospel is the belief that, through Christ's atonement, he has drawn God and men so closely together that forgiveness is possible for all. Therefore it is possible, also for all, to enter into that shining presence where God is, because, it is his will. As we stand, in this world here and now, we are like travellers across a great plain trying to see over the distant horizon. We cannot, because we are too small and our vision is too limited. All — and it is much — that we can do is rely upon the love of God, the promises of God, and the saving work of Christ.

A modern theologian, Professor M.F. Wiles, in *The Remaking of Christian Doctrine* puts it in another way:

'There does seem to be a fundamental inconsistency in the conception of a God whose purpose in creation includes as so prominent a feature the emergence of personal life capable of response to him, but whose purpose also allows for the utter extinction of those relationships of love, developed so gradually, so profoundly and yet with such tantalising incompleteness'.

And who shall we meet with in Heaven? We need to turn back to another century for a moving reply from Bishop Walsham How:

'Who has not some one loved and loving spirit waiting there — waiting for a blissful reunion — waiting to welcome the newly set free spirit to the joys of Paradise? Most of us have surely more than one such gone before us whom we hope to meet. Some of these are surely there — waiting for us, ready to welcome us, ready to make us feel as though we had come home, instead of gone into a strange land . . . Then welcome death! Welcome solemn messenger from our dear and loving Lord! Thou comest to call us away to joy and peace untold. Thou art but as the narrow stream which parts us from our promised land. Thou art but as the little golden gate which opens into Paradise'.

In the same century as How, the great preacher Henry Liddon of St Paul's, once at Advent in that Cathedral preached a sermon on the theme of 'The first five minutes after death'. In it he argued that the greatest adventure and the greatest revelation ever to be known to any man would be at such a time. Among the experiences would be, not only of entering into the presence of God, not only of seeing those whom we had longed to see again; but also that of seeing ourselves for the first time in wholeness and in truth:

'At our entrance on another world we shall know

our old selves as never before. The past will lie spread out before us, and we shall take a comprehensive survey of it. Each man's life will be displayed to him as a river, which he traces from its source in a distant mountain till it mingles with the distant ocean. The course of that river lies, sometimes through dark forests which hide it from view, sometimes through sands or marshes in which it seems to loose itself. Here it forces a passage angrily between the precipitous rocks, there it glides gently through meadows which it makes green and fertile. At one while it might seem to be turning backwards out of pure caprice; at another to be parting, like a gay spendthrift, with half its volume of water; while later on it receives contributory streams that restore its strength. And so it passes on, till the ebb and flow of the tides upon its bank tells that the end is near. What will not the retrospect be, when, after death, we survey, for the first time, as with a bird's eye view, the whole long range — the strange vicissitudes, the loss and gain, as we deem it, the failures and the triumphs of our earthly existence; when we measure it, as never before, in its completeness, now that it is at last over!'

He ends with these thrilling words; 'Those first five minutes, that first awakening to a new existence, with its infinite possibilities, will only be tolerable if we have indeed, with the hands of faith and love, laid hold on the hope set before us, in the person of Jesus Christ our Lord and Saviour . . . we may think calmly even of that tremendous experience, if he, the eternal God, is indeed our refuge, and underneath are the everlasting arms'.

But let the final word on this great matter of the life of the world to come be not with the great preachers, not with the philosophers, not with the scholars, or the scientists, but with a child. She was dying, the twelve year old girl of this story, and recently, in a London Children's Hospital. During the weeks of her illness she had learned to pick out a few simple tunes on a flute which her parents had given her. One afternoon, just before tea-time in the ward, she called to a nurse and said: 'When I go to be with Jesus, don't forget to pack my flute. I know he'll want to hear me play my tune'. Truly indeed did Christ say: 'Whoever does not receive the Kingdom of God like a child shall not enter it'.

When in distress

I believe that I shall see the goodness of the Lord in the land of the living! Wait for the Lord; be strong, and let your heart take courage; yea wait for the Lord!

Psalm 27:13:14

When in need of hope

Let thy steadfast love, oh Lord, be upon us, even as we hope in Thee.

Psalm 33:22

When in need of reassurance

God is our refuge and strength, a very present help in trouble. Therefore will we not fear though the earth should change, though the mountains shake in the heart of the sea; though its waters roar and foam, though the mountains tremble with its tumult . . . The Lord of Hosts is with us; the God of Jacob is our refuge.

Psalm 46 1:3:7

When in distress

Cast your burden on the Lord, and he will sustain you.

Psalm 55:22

When in affliction

Be merciful to me, oh God, be merciful to me, for in thee my soul takes refuge; in the shadow of thy wings I will take refuge, till the storms of destruction pass by.

Psalm 57:1

The most loved Psalm for those in sorrow

The Lord is my shepherd, I shall not want; he makes me lie down in green pastures. He leads me beside still waters, he restores my soul. He leads me in paths of righteousness for his name's sake. Even though I walk through the valley of the shadow of death, I fear no evil, for thou art with me; thy rod and they staff, they comfort me. Thou preparest a table before me in the presence of my enemies; thou anointest my head with oil, my cup overflows. Surely goodness and mercy shall follow me all the days of my life; and I shall dwell in the House of the Lord for ever.

Psalm 23

When in need of strength

Have you not known? Have you not heard? The Lord is the everlasting God, the creator of the ends of the earth. He does not faint or grow weary, his understanding is unsearchable. He gives power to the faint, and to him who has no might he increases strength. Even youths shall faint and be weary, and young men shall fall exhausted; but they who wait for the Lord shall renew their strength, they shall mount up with wings like eagles, they shall run and not be weary, they shall walk and not faint.

Isaiah 40 28:31

When in need of courage

Fear not, for I am with you, be not dismayed, for I am your God; I will strengthen you, I will help you, I will uphold you with my victorious right hand.

Isaiah 41:10

PRAYERS OF COMFORT, NEW AND OLD

The Christian hope

Almighty God, who didst raise from the dead our Lord Jesus Christ and did set him at thy right hand in the glory everlasting, I thank thee for this hope of immortality with which through many ages thou hast cheered and enlightened the souls of thy saints; and which thou didst most surely seal though the same Jesus Christ our Lord.

John Bailey

Now the God of hope fill us with all joy and peace in believing, that we may abound in hope through the power of the Holy Spirit; through him who died for us and rose again, Jesus Christ our Lord.

Based on Romans 15:13

Dying

O Lord Jesus Christ, who in thy last agony didst commend thy spirit into the hands of thy Heavenly Father, have mercy upon all sick and dying persons; may death be unto them the gate of everlasting life; and give the assurance of thy presence even in the dark valley; for thy name's sake who art the resurrection and the life, and to whom be glory forever.

Adapted from the Sarum Primer

Lord, I love you very much and really do want to be with you always, but I am afraid of dying. Give me the kind of faith in you that will not waver, the kind of hope which will help me to believe that you will be with me even to the end of the world, and the kind of love that will trust you completely whatever happens. Keep me in peace and guard me from fear, for the sake of you dear son who knows human frailty so well.

Michael Hollings: *The shade of His Hand*

Death

Oh Lord, support us all the day long of this troublous life, until the shades lengthen, and the evening comes, and the busy world is hushed, the fever of life is over, and our work is done. Then, Lord, in thy mercy, grant us safe lodging, a holy rest, and peace at the last; through Jesus Christ our Lord.

The 1928 Book of Common Prayer

Man dies, and this world dies; but nothing can bring your love to an end. Your love would grasp and hold us so that we too should outlive this world's tragedy.

Forgive us, that we have been frightened by death and parting, as if that were the final fact. Forgive us, that the nerve of our faith has broken; and that, seeing no definite answers, we have thought there was no answer, and have been overwhelmed by the futility of the things of this world. Forgive us, and let us see that you have touched your Kingdom with immortality, and called us into it. Through Jesus Christ, our Lord.

More Contemporary Prayers.   Edited Caryl Micklem

Bereavement

Lord, my loved ones are near me, I know that they live in the shadow. My eyes can't see them because they have left for a moment their bodies as one leaves behind outmoded clothing. Their souls, deprived of their disguise, no longer communicate with me. But in you, Lord, I hear them calling me. I see them beckoning to me. I hear them giving me advice. For they are now more vividly present. Before, our bodies touched but not our souls. Now I meet them when I meet you. I receive them when I receive you. I love them when I love you. Oh, my loved ones, eternally alive, who live in me, help me to learn thoroughly in this short life how to live eternally.

Prayers of Life. Michael Quoist

Lord, help me to realise that love does not cease when we die. Surely those I love who have died still go on loving me as they come to live more fully and deeply with God? Yet Lord, it is hard to understand. Our immediate loss makes us grieve, and forget that because of our union with you we are never separated from those who love you.

Michael Hollings. *The Shade of His Hand*

Life after Death

Oh Heavenly Father, help us to entrust our loved ones to thy care. When sorrow darkens our lives, teach us to look up to thee, remembering the cloud of witnesses by which we are compassed about. And grant that we on earth, rejoicing ever in thy presence, may share with them the rest and peace which thy presence gives; through Jesus Christ our Lord.

Canadian Prayer Book

Oh Lord our God, from whom neither life nor death can separate those who trust in thy love, and whose love holds in its embrace thy children in this world and in the next: so unite us to thyself that in fellowship with thee we may be always united to our loved ones whether here or there; give us courage, constancy, and hope; through him who died and was buried and rose again for us, Jesus Christ our Lord.

William Temple

SELECT BIBLIOGRAPHY

Autton, Norman *The Pastoral Care of the Dying* (SPCK 1966)

Autton, Norman *The Pastoral Care of the Bereaved* (SPCK 1967)

Barclay, William *Testament of Faith* (Mowbrays 1975)

Crichton, Ian *The Art of Dying* (Peter Owen 1976)

Dictionary of Medical Ethics (Darton, Longman and Todd)

Glover, Jonathan *Causing Death and Saving Lives* (Penguin Books 1977)

Hinton, John *Dying* (Penguin Books 1967)

Hollings, Michael *The Shade of His Hand* (Hodder & Stoughton 1973)

Jungel, Eberhard *Death, the Riddle and the Mystery* (St. Andrew Press 1975)

Kubler-Ross, Elizabeth *On Death and Dying* (Tavistock Publications 1977)

Parkes, Colin Murray *Bereavement* (Penguin Books 1976)

Perry, Michael *A Handbook of Parish Worship* (Mowbrays 1977)

Perry, Michael *The Resurrection of Man* (Mowbrays 1975)

Pincus, Lily *Death and the Family* (Faber and Faber 1976)

Saunders, Cicely *The Management of Terminal Illness* (Hospital Medicine Publications Ltd. 1967)